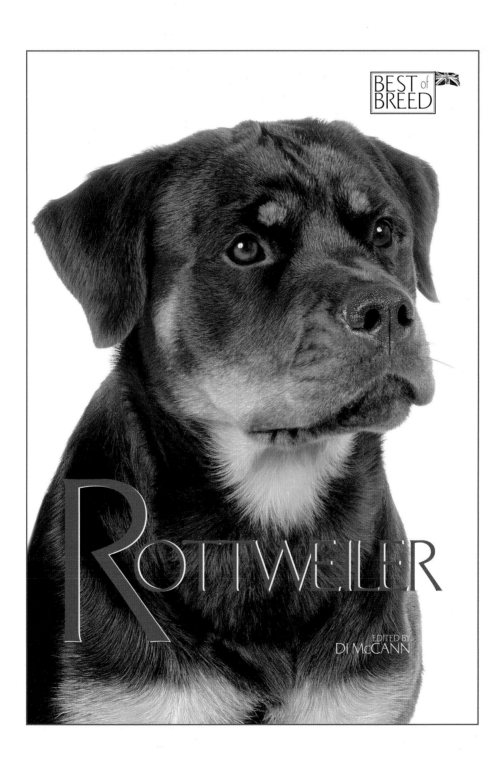

ROTTWEILER

EDITED BY
DI McCANN

This book is dedicated to the Rottweiler – past, present and future. From the early struggles of their foundation through their dramatic rise in popularity, they have had a punishing journey. Along the way they have given us knowledge and education, unquestioning loyalty and devotion. It is essential that we ensure the breed can continue its journey in safe hands.

ACKNOWLEDGEMENTS
The publishers would like to acknowledge the following for help with the publication: Pets As Therapy; Librarian Ciara Farrell, The Kennel Club; Dr. Manfred Herrmann, ADRK, Germany; Jan Cooper, American Rottweiler Club; American Kennel Club; Sussex Police; Kiene Zandbergen (Ter Waele Rottweilers); Mario Montes-Klaver (Munanis Rottweilers); Margaret Thomson; Di McCann (Parvenu); and Glynn Mulhall (Magglynn).

Cover photo: © Tracy Morgan Animal Photography (www.animalphotographer.co.uk)
page 2 © istockphoto.com/Eric Isselée; page 3 © istockphoto.com/Linda Loock
pages 21, 43, 129, 135 © istockphoto.com/Emmanuelle Bonzami
page 51 © istockphoto.com/Shadi Ejtemaee; page 53 © istockphoto.com/Brenda McEwan
page 55 © istockphoto.com/Serdar Yagci; page 92 © istockphoto.com/Brenda A. Smith;
page 119 © istockphoto.com/Waldemar Dabrowski; page 134 © istockphoto.com/Piotr Kozikowski

The British Breed Standard reproduced in Chapter 7 is the copyright of the Kennel Club and published with the club's kind permission. Extracts from the American Breed Standard are reproduced by kind permission of the American Kennel Club.

THE QUESTION OF GENDER
**The 'he' pronoun is used throughout this book instead of the rather impersonal 'it',
but no gender bias is intended.**

First published in 2008 by The Pet Book Publishing Company Limited
PO Box 8, Lydney, Gloucestershire GL15 6YD

ISBN
978-1-906305-10-9
1-906305-10-2

Printed and bound in Singapore.

CONTENTS

GETTING TO KNOW ROTTWEILERS

Chapter 1

So, you are considering acquiring a Rottweiler (pronounced rot-vile-er) and you want to know more about the breed. Or, perhaps, you already have one and you wish to expand on your knowledge. This book offers a no-nonsense approach to living with a Rottweiler in today's world. It will also show you the best ways of improving your knowledge and understanding of this wonderful, though sometimes much-maligned, breed.

The Rottweiler has suffered intense media pressure for a number of years due to some very tragic incidents. Since that time, however, owners and breeders have worked very hard to demonstrate the true qualities of this noble breed. Much more emphasis has been placed on training, socialising and the importance of breeding for sound

temperament, and, as a result, the Rottweiler's reputation has improved.

THE RIGHT OWNER
A Rottweiler is not for everyone. In the right hands he makes a wonderful companion or working dog, but the owner must understand the breed and be able to work with its unique qualities. Do not get a Rottweiler:
- **If you are unwilling to educate AND train your dog.** Basic obedience and household rules are not optional for the Rottweiler; they are essential! He is happiest when he has something to do. Attending a weekly training class is an ideal way of channelling his energy and enthusiasm.
- **If you lack leadership or you are unassertive.** If you think you might have difficulty asserting yourself calmly and confidently to exercise

leadership, or if you are a nervous or excitable person, choose a different breed that is known for its socially subordinate disposition.
- **If you dislike regular daily exercise.** A Rottweiler needs regular daily exercise to maintain health and muscle tone. You must take him out every day, usually twice a day, in all weathers! Do not get a Rottweiler unless you can commit yourself to this.
- **If you don't value constant companionship and sometimes physical affection!** The Rottweiler likes to be near people. He will follow you from room to room, always wanting to lay a head or paw on your lap, lean against you, or sit or stand on your feet. He will even force his head under your elbow, spilling your cup of tea, to insist that you fondle him.

The Rottweiler is a 'people dog' and is devoted to his human family.

- **If you are a fastidious or house-proud person.** The Rottweiler sheds his coat twice a year. He can sometimes slobber and can leave big, muddy footprints. A bitch will drop blood when in season. Think about this, especially if you have a white carpet or light-coloured furniture.
- **If you think that dogs should 'run free'.** With the Dangerous Dogs Act (1991) in the UK, our breed is under constant scrutiny by the authorities and the general public. An out-of-control or unsupervised Rottweiler is a 'no-no' in today's society. You must stay within the law and keep your dog under control, preferably keeping him on a lead in certain designated places. Even if you feel your dog is completely under control, consider what might happen if he encounters another, less well-behaved dog. Should the other dog start trouble, it is inevitably your dog that will get the blame because of the unfortunate reputation the breed has suffered, brought about by bad publicity and a handful of irresponsible owners.
- **If you are unwilling to share your house with a dog.** The Rottweiler's sole reason for being is to be included in the family unit, not shut outside in a kennel or enclosure. It is acceptable to leave a dog outside in a secure garden for part of the day, but the Rottweiler thrives on companionship and he will want to be wherever you are, sharing in your life and guarding you and your property.
- **If you cannot afford to provide proper food and veterinary care.** Owning a

If you take in a dog, you are responsible for his needs for the duration of his life.

Rottweiler is an expensive business. As a general rule, the larger the breed, the larger the food and veterinary bills. The Rottweiler can be prone to certain health problems (see Chapter 8) – these all cost money to treat.

- **If you are not prepared to put in 100 per cent supervision and care.** Although the Rottweiler's coat is short and easy to maintain, your dog will need to be brushed regularly and his ears, teeth and feet should be checked for problems. Do not leave a Rottweiler alone for long periods of time, as he can become bored and cause damage. He must be socialised, socialised, socialised with both dogs and humans and in all situations.

- **Unless you can commit yourself to the dog's entire lifetime.** The usual life span of a Rottweiler is about 9 to 12 years. If that seems too long a time for you to give unequivocal loyalty to your Rottweiler, please do not get one. Indeed, as most breeds have a life expectancy that is as long as this, if not longer, please don't get any dog!

If all the preceding 'bad news' about Rottweilers hasn't turned you away from the breed, by all means get a Rottweiler. They are every bit as wonderful as you have heard.

UNDERSTANDING THE BREED

Before you make up your mind about getting a Rottweiler (or, indeed, any breed of dog), you should really get to know the breed beforehand. Visit a breeder in your area who will allow you to mix with their dogs and answer your many questions, without badgering you into buying a puppy. A reputable breeder will always try to find time for the enthusiastic beginner. You will have a chance to see how you feel about the breed and whether you feel comfortable in the presence of these large and powerful dogs.

Dog shows are also a good way to observe numerous specimens and you will see well-behaved, and sometimes not-so-well-behaved, dogs. However, you will not get many opportunities to engage in meaningful discussion with owners of dogs at a show, as they are far too preoccupied with getting their dog ready to go into the ring in time for the class, rather than worrying about answering lots of questions. In addition to this, dogs behave more naturally in the home environment and this is what you really want to see.

The Rottweiler is a confident, self-assured dog who can be trained to a high level of obedience.

Generally speaking, the Rottweiler is good-natured, with a self-assured attitude. He is biddable and easily trained, sometimes to a high obedience standard. That said, the Rottweiler takes up to three years to mature, so if you acquire a puppy, be prepared to treat every day as a training day for the first few years.

Before going to the trouble and expense of seeking out your Rottweiler puppy, you must bear one thing in mind – the Rottweiler needs quality time. Quality time means making time to learn and play together, developing a positive rapport with your dog. It is imperative that you channel the Rottweiler's considerable energy into some form of play or obedience training. The energy has to go somewhere – if it does not, it may be channelled towards your possessions or your home as the dog becomes destructive, disobedient, hyperactive or even aggressive. The majority of people who own this breed have spent many hours developing their dog's character to produce a stable, sensible animal. This doesn't happen overnight – it takes time and patience.

The Rottweiler is probably best known for his inherent guarding instincts. He will defend his territory, sometimes quite vocally. However, the Rottweiler does not bark unnecessarily, and, when he does, it is usually for a reason, which should be investigated. The Rottweiler does not need to be encouraged to 'guard' – he will do

A powerfully built dog, the Rottweiler is compact and muscular.

this instinctively as he matures.

The Rottweiler has a habit of growling and grumbling in a non-aggressive fashion. In the vast majority of cases, this is a totally acceptable and endearing trait, which most owners will confirm. However, it can be a bit disconcerting for people unfamiliar with the breed. Sometimes, people will try to prove they aren't nervous around a Rottweiler by roughing them up around the head and ears, patting them around the body a bit too enthusiastically, or being a bit over-zealous when stroking the dog's head. Some Rottweilers are particularly sensitive around the

head and ears and resent this rough handling – wouldn't you? The best way to approach a Rottweiler on first encounter is not to stroke him over the head and ears, but to stroke him under his chin, then up and down his chest.

If you are already the proud owner of a Rottweiler, hopefully you will have studied the breed and observed it, before you took the plunge. The following chapters will give you a greater insight into the Rottweiler, as you want to enjoy many happy years together and nothing builds a better bond than trust and mutual understanding.

PHYSICAL CHARACTERISTICS

The Rottweiler is a medium- to large-sized, strong and powerful dog with a compact and muscular body. The adult male weighs about 42-52kg (92.5-114.5lb), while an adult female weighs about 35-42kg (77-92.5lb). The Rottweiler is a black-and-tan breed, which means that, as a result of the breed's genetic make-up, the tan markings are in exactly the same position as on every other black-and-tan breed (i.e. the Dobermann, Gordon Setter, American Cocker Spaniel, Manchester Terrier, and Lancashire Heeler). The tan

A Rottweiler will bond strongly with his owner, and will respect good, strong leadership.

colouring appears over the Rottweiler's eyes, around the muzzle and cheeks, across the chest on the legs and feet, and under the tail. White is sometimes seen on the Rottweiler's chest, as a result of the breed's genetic relationship to the Sennenhunds, but these white markings are considered a fault and would be penalised in the show ring. However, for the pet owner this is not particularly important, though neither is it ideal. The Rottweiler's coat is generally short, waterproof, and coarse to the touch, without wave or curls. Occasionally, long-coated dogs are seen (which look similar in appearance to the Bernese Mountain Dog), but this is also a fault.

The Rottweiler is described as a 'head breed', which means that the sum of all the parts of its head – the ear-set, the width of the skull, the depth of the stop (the forehead), the length and width of the muzzle – make up the whole expression, which is the unique quality of the breed and is instantly recognisable (rather like a blunt triangle).

The Rottweiler is very strong and sound in mind and body. He should convey an impression of endurance and purpose, covering the ground in a trotting style and in a short time; his movement should appear positive and effortless, without lameness or a stilted gait. Being a robust and active breed, the Rottweiler requires a considerable amount of exercise to keep him in good condition and to prevent him from becoming bored. Daily walks, as previously mentioned, and swimming when possible, will help keep him in good shape. For more information about appearance and physical attributes, see Chapter 7.

ARE YOU A PACK LEADER?

If you possess the quality of calm assertiveness, in all probability you will make a good pack leader. The Rottweiler is not a dog that enjoys challenges of strength from the man of the house, as this can result in the Rottweiler showing the dominant side of his character – which is when things can go wrong. This attitude from the man of the household is not calm assertiveness – it is male dominance and aggressiveness (in the eyes of the dog).

Just like humans, there are stages in canine development. When the Rottweiler reaches 12-18 months of age the owner may notice that their dog has become a little more challenging than usual. This may be particularly noticeable with a male. You can compare this to the adolescent male who behaves rather like a 'lager lout' and who thinks that he is big enough to speak back to his parents. This is natural behaviour and is to be expected with the males; less so with the females. These 'tantrums' must be dealt with firmly but kindly until your Rottweiler realises that you are, and will remain, pack leader. If a male Rottweiler is encouraged to accept this by the

time he is 18 months, barring something unforeseeable, you will have a well-behaved dog for life – literally eating out of the palm of your hand. The Rottweiler will willingly adapt to the house rules if the rules and training are consistent and the dog understands what he is and is not allowed to do.

With the Rottweiler it is essential to discourage what is referred to as 'mouthing', which should not be allowed under any circumstances. . People unfamiliar with the breed can sometimes interpret mouthing as a 'bite', and, if allowed to continue into adulthood, this innocent action could indeed develop into biting. Do not let this happen.

Mouthing is relatively easy to

eliminate. When a pup is with his littermates they play roughly and bite each other quite hard. Puppies at play are quite aggressive towards each other, until they realise the level of the bite that hurts the other puppy; it is at this point that the 'bitten' puppy will say 'that's enough!' – then the biting puppy learns to let go or a fight develops. This is called 'bite inhibition' and this is how puppies learn not to put too much pressure into their bite.

Until a puppy learns otherwise, he will exert the same pressure on you. When the pup grabs your hand or arm with teeth like sharp needles, do not snatch your hand or arm away quickly. Instead, let your puppy know it is hurting you by

In a litter, puppies will play roughly with each other – until one of them has had enough.

emitting a low growl or an "uh, uh" or "aaagh", try to lift the jaws gently and take away the hand or arm. Over a period of time the puppy will learn to lessen the pressure, although this requires kindness and patience from the owner.

When trying to eliminate mouthing behaviour, it is important not to get the puppy overexcited by screeching or screaming when it 'bites', as this will make matters worse; or the puppy will turn it into a game. It is totally unnecessary to use harsh methods to cure this very common problem. It must also be remembered that, when a puppy is teething (losing his 'baby' teeth as the permanent teeth come through), his gums will be sore and this also causes him to mouth and chew objects. If you are having problems controlling mouthing as a result of teething, seek the advice of your puppy's breeder who should always be on call for you. If your breeder cannot help, seek out an experienced breeder/owner who can help you. Mouthing is too important an issue to ignore, because unless it is dealt with at the outset, this innocent action could turn into a full bite when the dog is adult. It is totally unacceptable for an adult dog to mouth hands, arms or any part of clothing, however endearing it might seem. Be prepared to warn well-intentioned visitors who come to see the new puppy, to ensure they do not encourage the puppy to mouth.

TAILS – THEY WIN!

The Rottweiler was traditionally a docked breed until April 2007, when the Animal Welfare Act became law in the UK. The historical reasons for docking (amputation of the tail) are not specific. There are several suggestions, including the possible belief of the early Romans that the practice prevented rabies. Another historical suggestion is that, in some areas, dogs used for work were not taxed, so the owners of such dogs would dock the tails to indicate that the dog was used for work and therefore not subject to a tax. Farmers were taxed according to the length of their dogs' tails, so docking was used to reduce the tax liability. A further notion was that, because hunting for sport was considered to be reserved for the wealthy nobility, only long-tailed dogs were suitable for hunting. As such, the owners of long-tailed dogs were required to pay a high tax and therefore tail docking became a practice of the commoners.

In more modern times docking was continued because of tradition at dog shows. Docking for purely cosmetic reasons has been banned in some Scandinavian countries since 1989. In the Rottweiler's native Germany – and in most of Europe – docking has been banned since 1998. The news of the ban in the UK became more popular with the majority of the puppy-buying public, as they were previously not aware that they had a choice of having a puppy with a tail intact. Some people believed that keeping tails on the Rottweiler would give them a more 'approachable' look and soften public opinion of a breed that had suffered unkind sensationalism from the media and the public alike.

Humans, as well as dogs, read a dog's temperament by the position and carriage of the tail, as well as the head and ears. So, a natural, wagging tail will add to the Rottweiler's reputation as a truly benevolent and self-assured guardian of the family.

TAIL CARRIAGE

Normal tail carriage at rest: This dog is happy and relaxed.

Tail carriage changes when the dog is interested or excited.
Photos courtesy: Munanis Rottweilers.

A sense of mutual respect must be established between a Rottweiler and younger members of his human family.

FAMILY LIFE

CHILDREN
A Rottweiler is usually tolerant of children, provided the children have been taught to treat the Rottweiler with respect and kindness, and they are not allowed to tease the dog. Some Rottweilers resent the occasional rough treatment children can inflict, so it is up to the parents to ensure this does not happen. Being quite a large dog, the Rottweiler's naturally exuberant nature and enthusiasm for games can sometimes lead to children being knocked over as they join in the fun. Also, the Rottweiler's nails can sometimes scratch a child inadvertently during play. Therefore, as with any breed of dog, playtime with children and Rottweilers must be carefully

supervised. Children must learn to allow the dog to have quiet time away from the rest of the family, and they must always be supervised if they are near the dog when he is feeding. Brought up correctly in a firm and fair manner, Rottweilers are a wonderful addition to any family. However (like any other dog), a Rottweiler must never be left alone with babies or children at any time.

OTHER ANIMALS
A Rottweiler will generally accept the presence of other animals and pets without too much fuss, provided they are introduced in a calm and safe environment. The dog must not be allowed to chase or worry smaller animals. The Rottweiler has a high 'prey drive' and will naturally chase small

furry animals, so he must learn not to do this. He can live comfortably alongside other breeds of dog and to take his place within the pack hierarchy. However, he is a dominant breed and will tend to want the top spot, so problems can arise in a multi-dog household if you aren't careful. Fights can and do happen, especially between the bitches around 'season' time, when they can be quite territorial; or with the males if one of them has been used at stud. However, do not confuse his dominant or belligerent manner towards other dogs with an aggressive attitude towards people – the former is part of the Rottweiler's ingrained character; the latter is due to bad breeding or lack of socialisation and is totally unacceptable.

The Rottweiler is the chosen breed for the Austrian Army.

Photo courtesy: Ter Waele Rottweilers.

THE VERSATILE ROTTWEILER

One of the best things about the Rottweiler is his exceptional versatility. As well as being a much-loved family companion and exhibited worldwide in the show ring, he is used as a working dog in many services all over the world and competes with great success in many canine sports.

WORKING DOGS

The working abilities of the Rottweiler have evolved from the breed's original purpose. In antiquity, the Roman army needed to move cattle to feed the thousands of soldiers on their conquering marches through Europe. The ancestors of today's Rottweiler were used to move the cattle during marching as well as guarding the animals overnight. When these services were no longer required by the Romans, the Rottweiler became a droving dog, helping the local butcher to move his cattle to and from local markets; and he was also used to pull small carts carrying milk churns. These traits are still inherent in the Rottweiler today, and in some countries herding and carting rallies and competitions are held, in which the Rottweiler performs extremely well.

The Rottweiler's natural scenting skills and guarding instincts have also been put to good use in a number of other fields. The Austrian Army has used Rottweilers since 1964, when a Rottweiler breeding programme was introduced. In Switzerland the Rottweiler's excellent scenting abilities are utilised by Customs, while in Norway there are many Rottweilers used in Search and Rescue. Furthermore, the Rottweiler is a popular choice among police forces the world over.

The Rottweiler has worked in Scandinavia for many years in the search and rescue of human survivors and dead bodies in deep snow, where their great scenting skills are used most successfully. To do this work the Rottweiler must have not only a good nose and an active, healthy body, but also a calm and benevolent disposition to be able to cope with stressed or injured survivors that have been found. Today, there are training clubs in most parts of Scandinavia specifically set up to teach the

The Rottweiler is used by police forces worldwide. This is police dog Olsen.
Photo courtesy: Sussex Police.

The Rottweiler will usually be seen at either of these events and their owners will be more than happy to tell you how to train your dog to such a level in order that you may compete too. The Kennel Club will also be able to provide you with more information about clubs in your area.

Working trials is another area in which the Rottweiler has had success in competition. In the UK, this is a very popular outdoor sport. To be successful, dogs and handlers must work as a team. There are five phases through which the dog must pass progressively. These levels are known as 'stakes' and each stake increases in difficulty. The stakes are: Companion Dog, Utility Dog, Working Dog, Tracking Dog and Patrol Dog (see Chapter 6 for further information).

Schutzhund is another popular sport in which many Rottweilers participate, particularly in the breed's native Germany. The name comes from the German word meaning 'protection dog'. Schutzhund originated in Germany to test the temperament and ability of the German Shepherd Dog, ensuring only quality dogs were bred from. Today it is practised worldwide. There are three disciplines involved in Schutzhund – tracking, obedience and protection. In effect, Schutzhund is a 'triathlon' for working dogs, and, as a result of his working heritage, the Rottweiler acquits himself very well in this sport.

Rottweiler and other breeds of dogs this vital work.

SPORTING DOGS

Most people are familiar with dog shows such as Crufts in the UK or Westminster in the US, which are usually televised. What is less well known is that the Rottweiler competes in many other canine disciplines, such as tracking, agility, obedience, working trials and Schutzhund, with great success.

There are obedience and agility clubs throughout the UK that hold training sessions to help people educate and train their dogs. They also hold shows during the summer months and many people take their dogs to shows up and down the country.

THERAPY ROTTWEILERS

The health and psychological benefits of contact with animals are becoming increasingly well understood, and, as a result, therapy dogs are more in demand than ever.

Therapy Dogs are assessed and vaccinated animals, owned by registered volunteers who make pre-arranged visits to hospitals, hospices, residential care homes, day centres, special needs schools and many other establishments, providing comfort, companionship and therapeutic care to patients and residents. The animals and their owners have to pass a strict assessment before qualifying. Therapy Dogs are also trained to be of assistance to the blind, deaf and physically handicapped who may be housebound. In the UK, the leading therapy dog organisation is Pets As Therapy (PAT).

At nearly nine years of age, Becky is a PAT dog who visits a home for the elderly, a home for people with learning disabilities, and attends outings for handicapped children. She won PAT Dog of the Year in 2006.

AN IDEAL HOME: TOWN OR COUNTRY?

The quality of ownership is far more important than where a dog lives. Having said that, a high-rise flat is really not the best place to keep a Rottweiler, especially when you are trying to toilet train a young puppy, which would have to be carried up and down stairs, or taken in a lift.

It is a challenge to keep a large

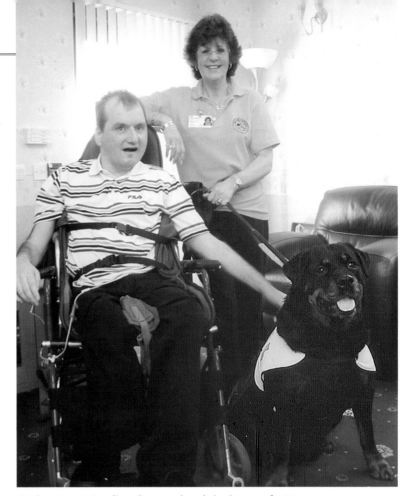

Becky: An outstanding therapy dog, bringing comfort to many.

dog in the city. A city Rottweiler needs an owner who remains calm and sensitive to his needs and can help him to learn to stay calm too, in all situations (people can become very uptight around Rottweilers). Providing that a Rottweiler has been bred for soundness and temperament, however, he can be an excellent dog for city life. He is confident and balanced when bred and socialised correctly, which makes him secure enough to walk among traffic and people, with all of the varied noises that exist in a city. Most public parks within a city are ideal for exercising your

Rottweiler and are also great places for socialisation, as you have everything there – tourists, locals, people of different ages, sizes and ethnic backgrounds, people in wheelchairs, cyclists, joggers, footballers, ducks, squirrels, builders, and even horses and brass bands. Don't forget to take your poop scoop bag with you to clear up your dog's mess.

All dogs should have access to an outside space in order to relieve themselves first thing in the morning and last thing at night, and this is especially important for puppies. If your

MALE OR FEMALE?

Whichever sex you decide on, your Rottweiler will make a loyal and faithful companion to the family, as both sexes thrive on human companionship.

The male Rottweiler is bigger, heavier and stronger than the female and can be more arrogant. He needs a firmer hand and is not suitable for those inexperienced with dogs of strong character, or people of a nervous disposition. Many breeders will not sell a male to first-time dog owners or those who have not owned large breeds before. The males can, and do, urinate in the home (marking their territory) unless specifically trained or encouraged not to do so. Once they have learned the house rules, however, a male Rottweiler can be 'putty in your hand' until the day he dies.

Female Rottweilers are usually easier to handle, although sometimes they can be dominant over other dogs in the house. Their guarding instincts are just as high as the males'. Females come 'in season' usually every six months and will drop blood during this time. However, they are cleaner than males in the house, if taught properly. They are generally thought to be more responsive to the younger members of the household and are particularly gentle around children and the elderly.

Please beware of the breeder who is willing to sell you two puppies from the same litter. This is usually not a good idea, as the puppies will tend to bond with each other instead of with you. If you leave the puppies on their own for long periods of time, they will play together, which will lead inevitably to fighting and, as a result, the destruction of things around them, i.e. furniture, books, clothing, toys etc. You will find when you take them out together and let them off the lead, that they will chase each other about and then totally ignore your calls to get them back. Each puppy needs quality time with his new owner in order to respond effectively to training sessions. If you must have two, wait until the first one is at least six months old before getting another.

There is a significant difference in size between males and females when they are fully grown.

garden is very small, or you don't have one, this need not be a problem as long as you are prepared to take your dog outside, and at least your dog will have regular road walks to keep him fit and healthy.

If you live in the suburbs and have a garden, or you live in the countryside with lots of public footpaths, then you are indeed fortunate. You will have plenty of opportunities to exercise your Rottweiler. However, he should not be left to run free and annoy other users of the countryside. He must be taught not to chase farm animals, and of course you must always remember to shut farm and field gates. Nothing is nicer than a well-behaved Rottweiler trotting beside you on a lead, along a country lane, but he must learn to be quiet and well behaved when passing horse riders or bike-riders, or other dogs and their owners.

Living in a quiet rural area where there are perhaps not so many other families with dogs means that you will have to put more effort into socialising your young Rottweiler with people, children and other breeds of dogs, and also traffic. This is not such a difficult thing to do, as you will probably live not too far from a supermarket where your dog can be familiarised with squeaky trollies, push-bikes, screaming children or babies, old people with sticks, lorries and buses with noisy airbrakes.

Regardless of whether you have acres of countryside at your disposal or simply a local park, exercise is vital for your Rottweiler

The Rottweiler needs regular and varied exercise.

and you should aim for a lean, fit dog – not a fat, flabby, overweight couch-potato. Regular exercise, twice a day, is best. This also helps to keep the Rottweiler's mind active, as well as his body, which helps to prevent him from becoming bored about the home, causing damage. Control of your dog is an absolute must, and, by having a well-controlled Rottweiler on the end of the lead, you will be helping to change the public's perception of this oft-misunderstood breed.

Wherever you live, please remember that your dog should not be allowed to run up to other dogs. You should let your Rottweiler off the lead only if he has a solid recall and can respond immediately when another dog turns up.

AN ACTIVE LIFESTYLE

If you love to walk or jog, the Rottweiler will happily accompany you. Most Rottweilers enjoy swimming, and, if you are extremely lucky and live near a safe river, or if you own your own swimming pool with a shallow walk-in, your Rottweiler will enjoy many hours of swimming beside you and joining in the fun – particularly retrieving water toys.

If you truly understand what is involved in taking on a large dog with a strong guarding instinct and a strong character, and if you are an active person with an active lifestyle who wants a dog to join in your daily activities, a Rottweiler could be just the dog for you.

THE FIRST ROTTWEILERS

Chapter 2

Although the actual history of the Rottweiler begins in Roman history, the development of the breed we know today began with his use by cattle dealers and butchers as a guard and drover's dog. At that time he would have had to be versatile and rugged, with sufficient stamina to drive, guard and keep the cattle under control without dispersing them. He would need to manipulate obstinate bulls, and, at the same time, be alert and watchful for his master on lonely and dangerous roads. He would undoubtedly have slept outside, so he would have needed a weatherproof topcoat and plenty of undercoat. Without all these traits the dealers and butchers would have achieved very little. Is it any wonder, therefore, that the following characteristics, taken from the Breed Standard (see

Chapter 7), provide an accurate description of our breed: *above average size, stalwart, compact and powerful, endurance trotter, bold and courageous, self-assured and fearless?*

Nothing unites man and dog more than working together every day, which is where undesirable traits of cowardice, inattention and lack of discipline would be highlighted. In order to produce a fully dependable and watchful cattle-droving dog, those that did not meet the standard were weeded out of the gene pool.

The history books of our breed tell us that the Romans conquered most of Europe and they probably kept a tough, but agile, dog to drove and herd the cattle needed to feed the armies on their conquering marches. These dogs would have kept the cattle safe from the predators of the time (bears, wolves etc). Without adequate documentation

or proof, however, we can only surmise that, perhaps over several centuries, these early dogs would have mixed with the local mountain dogs, gradually watering down the two extremes and producing an animal of courage and sturdiness but with a willingness to work.

The town of Rottweil – from where our breed derives its name – dates back to the year 73 or 74 AD when the 11th Legion of the Roman Empire laid out a camp on the bank of the Neckar river in the Württemberg area of Germany. The Romans' love of luxurious villas, complete with heated baths made of mosaics, is well known. It is believed that later excavations unearthed the red tiles and bricks of these villas, and the area became known as 'das Rote Wil'. The red roof tiles gave it the first half of its name 'rot', while its origin as a Roman city gave it 'wil' for

The Rottweiler performing his original role, driving cattle.

Photo courtesy: Carol Delsman.

villa. So, from the city of red-roofed Roman villas evolved the name 'Rottweil'.

Rottweil developed as an important trade centre for grain and livestock, and the cattle traders encouraged the development of a sturdy breed of dog similar to that which we know today. Endemic to the harsher regions of the Italian and Swiss Alps is the group of dogs known as the Sennenhunds – the traditional Swiss herding breeds – which is why it is believed that Rottweilers are cousins not only of the large Molosser breeds but also of the Sennenhunds (which include the Bernese Mountain Dog, Greater Swiss Mountain Dog, Appenzeller and Entlebucher). The Rottweiler's similarity to these breeds is

testament to that. The need to control cattle, including dangerous bulls, probably meant that dogs of the bulldog or bullenbeisser type may have been brought into the breeding plans in order to produce the massive jaw structure that today gives the Rottweiler such a powerful bite. These bold dogs became known as the Rottweiler Metzgerhund (Butcher's Dog of Rottweil) and would be seen safeguarding their masters' profits in a leather purse tied around their necks.

Other words used to describe the Rottweiler's character include: '*Good natured, not nervous; biddable, with natural guarding instincts,*' which is why the Rottweiler's versatile nature meant that he could also be harnessed to a small cart for the

butcher, the milkman, the baker and anyone else who used carts for transporting their wares to market. With the advent of the railway, however, driving cattle by dogs was forbidden and donkeys replaced dogs as draft animals, so dogs' carting skills became redundant. But this trait is still in evidence today in America and Canada, where popular carting rallies and competitions are held regularly.

In 1899, the International Club for Leonbergers and Rottweiler Dogs was formed in Germany, and, in fact, the first Breed Standard for the Rottweiler was produced by this club in 1901. Unfortunately, this club eventually died out and two other clubs, exclusively for the Rottweiler, were formed. The DRK (Deutscher Rottweiler-Klub

The butcher's dog: A drawing by Czechoslovakian Dagmar Cernar, depicting a butcher and his dog.

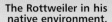

The Rottweiler in his native environment.

– German Rottweiler Club) was founded on 13 January 1907 in Heidelberg, followed by the creation of the SDRK (Süddeutscher Rottweiler-Klub – South German Rottweiler Club) on 26 April of the same year. A third club was quickly formed, the Internationale Rottweilerklub, which took over from the SDRK, and the two clubs operated side by side until 14 August 1921, when they merged to become the ADRK (Allgemeiner Deutscher Rottweiler Klub) now known as the official German Rottweiler club. The slogan of the ADRK was and still remains: Die Rottweilerzucht ist und bleibt Gebrauchshundezucht (the breeding of Rottweilers is and shall be the breeding of working dogs).

It seems fitting that this book is written in the centenary year of the ADRK. Enthusiasts, judges and breeders from around the world gathered in Rottweil on 18 and 19 August 2007, for the Klubsiegerzuchtschau (the main Rottweiler breed show), where a total of 628 dogs, from 33 nations, were entered. The following weekend the IFR (International Friends of the Rottweiler) Working (Schutzhund) Championships were also held in Rottweil. Many people crowded the small town and stayed the whole week to support both events, which made it a very memorable centenary celebration.

EARLY ROTTWEILERS

As can be seen from these four photographs found in old books, these dogs look very different to each other. This is because the Rottweiler in its native Germany varied greatly during the early years of its development at or around the beginning of the 20th century, as the breeders were trying to establish a certain "type". Establishing "type" in a breed means achieving a certain consistency of how the dog looks, within its own breed, as compared to another breed, e.g. the Dobermann. However, it was not until after World War II that the breeding of Rottweilers really began to take shape as breeders in Germany strived to produce better-looking animals, with a sound working ability who would be able to win at the prestigious ADRK club show. So, compare the photographs on pages 26, 27 and 28 to those on page 33 and you can begin to see how breeders have drastically controlled "type" over a number of years.

Leo v Cannstatt.

Lord Remo v Schifferstadt.

Lord vd Teck.

Odo v Gaisburg.

The Rottweiler in the police service.

Lord Remo v Schifferstadt: German Rottweiler dog winner 1913.

Leo von Overstricht, born 3 February 1911.

The winner of the Breeder Group – 'vom Kohlerwald' – at the Dortmund Winners show 11-12 June 1932.

A female winner of pure breeding.

Sieger Hackel von Kohlerwald.

THE ROTTWEILER IN THE UK

There is no trace of Rottweilers being imported or registered with the Kennel Club in the UK prior to 1936, when the breed's first pioneer, Mrs Phil (Thelma) Gray of the Rozavel kennels (famous for her Alsatians and Corgis), registered a bitch imported from Germany called **Rozavel Diana von der Amalienburg SchH I** born 25 May 1934 (*Sire: Hackel vom Köhlerwald SchHII – Dam: Alma von Hartmannshofen*). Breeder: Herr Vincenz Heim (Jnr.). Diana was said to be a very lovely bitch and records show that she was the first Rottweiler bitch to be imported into the UK.

At first, Rottweilers were not registered in their own right with the Kennel Club, but were instead to be found in the section of The *Kennel Gazette* entitled: 'Any Other Breed or Variety of British, Colonial or Foreign Dog Not Classified', originals of which are held at the Kennel Club library in London.

With the help of the ADRK, Mrs Gray imported again and registered a male in September 1936. This was **Rozavel Arnolf von der Entinger Ruine** born 30 January 1936 (*Sire: Bruno von der Burghalde – Dam: Bella von der Kaltental*). Breeder: Herr Simon Odermatt. Arnold was a very good specimen and was exhibited at Crufts in 1937, where he went Best of Breed; he won five awards at other shows and also did very well in the obedience ring.

In November 1936 Diana was subsequently sold and transferred into the ownership of a Mrs Simmons of Crowsteps kennel. In the Change of Name section of the *Kennel Gazette* dated November 1936, she appears as **Crowsteps Diana von der**

Amalienburg. Mrs Simmons did quite well with her in obedience and working trials, gaining CD and UD qualifications. Mrs Simmons also exhibited her at Crufts in 1937 in the Novice class (dog or bitch), where there were just five entries.

Mrs Simmons mated Diana to Rozavel Arnolf and the litter was born on 25 October 1937. Three males (Crowsteps Davall, also Diaz, Donner) and five females (Delia, Daun, Dieta, Dirne, Doro) were registered in the *Kennel Gazette* dated January 1938. Nothing further is recorded of this litter.

In the *Kennel Gazette*, July 1936, a bitch was registered by a Miss E.M. Paton of Great Bookham in the name of **Kingsmark Enne von Pfalzgau** born 1 March 1933 (*Sire: Dago vom Stadweiler – Dam: Anni von Pfalzgau*). Breeder: Herr

Thelma Gray pictured with her prize-winning Rottweilers in 1936.

Int. Ch.Rozavel Vefa von Kohlerwald.

Weirmann. Enne had been imported in whelp to the World Champion Ido von Köhlerwald SchH II. A litter of seven was born in quarantine on 18 June 1936, and three bitches were registered with the Kennel Club; these were Kingsmark Alma, Else from Rozavel and Anna von Rozavel – sadly, all but one died of distemper.

The surviving bitch puppy, Anna von Rozavel, won Best of Breed at Crufts in 1939. She was trained by a Mr Montgomery and turned out to be a very good working dog, qualifying CDex in working trials. She was a very accomplished bitch, winning on 36 occasions, both in trials and in the show ring. Due to the outbreak of World War II in 1939, Anna was commissioned by the army and stayed with her handler until she died at the age of 16 years. As a result she was

never used for breeding.

During the latter half of 1936, Mrs Gray again imported a bitch in whelp to the famous Sieger Hackel von Köhlerwald SchH II - born 1929 (*Sire: Alfon (Brendle) SchHII – Dam: Anny von der Lauter*). She was registered as **Rozavel Asta von Norden** born 23 June 1934 (*Sire: Bruno von der Burghalde – Dam: Alma (Nikolaus*). Breeder: Herr Karl-Rohm. The litter was born on 23 August 1936 – four males (Hans from Rozavel, also Helmuth, Hermann and Herzog) and four bitch puppies (Hedda, Hedwig, Hexe, Hilde). Mrs Gray also mated Arnolf to Asta and produced six males (Iago from Rozavel, also Ibsen, Ich Dien, Igor, Inbrunst, Inhaber) and three female puppies (Imelda, Ingwer, Isis) born on 4 September 1937. However, nothing further is known of these two litters.

In June 1937, Kingsmark Enne von Pfalzgau had been transferred from the ownership of Miss Paton to Mrs Thelma Gray, and with Enne now in her ownership, Mrs Gray mated her to Arnolf. The resulting litter of nine males (Jager of Rozavel, also Jakob, Joshua, Julius, Junge, Jungling, Junker, Jurist, Jux) and four females (Jacqueline, Johanna, Juliana, Juliette) were born on 30 October 1937.

Mrs Gray then imported a really outstanding bitch from Germany; she was registered in the July 1937 *Kennel Gazette* as **International Champion Rozavel Vefa vom Köhlerwald Ztp** born on 9 May 1934 (*Sire: Arno von Zenthof SchH III (Fels von Stuttgart/Arka) – Dam: Aga vom Lederberg (Hackel vom Köhlerwald/Xanta von Gaisburg*). Breeder: Mr E. Weber. Vefa had been mated to Lump von

Captain F. Roy Smith with the first post-war imports: Ajax von Fuhrenkamp and Berny von Weyher.

Lotte von Osterburg.

Hohenreissach (*Sire: Igo von Köhlerwald – Dam: Dora vom Hohenreissach*) before she came into quarantine where she produced a large litter of 12 puppies, born on 30 March 1937. The litter was registered at the Kennel Club in July 1937 – four males (Ido of Rozavel, also Imp, Ink, Ito) and eight females (Iga, Ila, Ima, Ina, Ira, Iso, Ita, Iti). Sadly, disaster struck again and all the puppies died. How disappointing that a bitch with Vefa's qualities should have left no mark here.

Mrs Simmons imported a male from Germany, whose registration appeared in the October 1937 *Kennel Gazette* as **Crowsteps Arbo von Gaisburg** born 11 April 1937 (*Sire: Ulrich von Gaisburg (Lord von Gaisburg/Britta von Gaisburg) – Dam: Astra von der Burghalde (Fels von Stuttgart/Flora von Weil)*). Breeder: Herr Jacob Kopf. It appears from the records

of January 1940 that Arbo sired a litter to Jacqueline from Rozavel (a bitch from the Arnolf to Enne litter). One bitch puppy owned by a Mrs S. Mulcaster was registered in the name of Portholme Elizabeth (born 23 April 1939 – breeder: Miss N. Morris). Apparently, Arbo was a good obedience worker but nothing further is recorded of his daughter, Portholme Elizabeth.

When her home was requisitioned by the Canadian Army for the war effort, Mrs Gray sent her remaining Rottweilers over to Ireland for safe-keeping. After the war, attempts were made to find them and return them to England, but they had vanished without a trace. It is so very sad that despite all Mrs Gray's efforts, she was unable to construct an on-going breeding programme for Rottweilers in the United Kingdom at that time.

The tenacity and gallant efforts

of these pre-war breeders cannot go without mention. To have made the commitment to name and register the puppies, and then to lose litters in the way that they did (probably with distemper, which was rife at the time, despite a vaccine to combat the disease) must have been heart-breaking. With an imminent war, we know for sure that many owners had their dogs euthanased, rather than have them go through the terrifying atmosphere of the bombings.

Due to World War II, no registrations were recorded between the years 1941-1952 inclusive. Between the years 1953 and 1964, Kennel Club records show 198 Rottweiler registrations.

POST-WAR BREEDING
In his book *Dogs in Britain*, published in 1948, canine librarian and author Clifford L.B.

Hubbard wrote, *"There have been no importations within recent years, and the original stock is becoming too old for breeding; thus the future for the Rottweiler in Britain is not very bright, which is unfortunate as the breed is invaluable as an all-round obedience dog and an excellent guard."* Mr Hubbard need not have worried.

Captain Frederick Roy-Smith had been a young veterinary surgeon serving with the army of occupation in Germany in the Royal Army Veterinary Corps when he came across the Rottweiler in the course of his duties. He was so impressed by the breed's working capabilities that, when he left the service, he returned to Germany and brought back Ajax and Berny, who entered Britain in March 1953.

Ajax von Führenkamp born on 20 April 1952 (Sire: Baldur von Alt-Trauchberg – Dam: Cilly vom Solastrand). Breeder: Wilhelm Drevenstedt. Ajax was the first stud dog imported into the UK. Ajax was shown at Crufts in 1955 and gained a third place in an Any Other Variety class.
Berny von Weyher was born on 11 June 1952 (Sire: Barri von der Steinlachburg – Dam: Frigga vom Leinetal). Breeder: Mrs P. Voigt. Although Ajax and Berny were registered in the *Kennel Gazette* of September 1953, Berny had not been registered with the ADRK, as she was long-coated and not a first-class specimen. Furthermore,

Rintelna the Bombardier CDex, UDex: Sire of the first British Champion.

she was not a good brood bitch and she did not produce a puppy of good enough quality. Apparently, Ajax was mated to Berny a total of six times, producing four pups. However, all died except one, which was sold as a pet and never heard of again.

Captain Roy-Smith imported another bitch, **Lotte von Osterburg**, registered in the 1955 *Kennel Gazette* as Rintelna Lotte von Osterburg, born 2 February 1952 (Sire: Arras von der Schweizergrenze – Dam: Bella vom Klosterhof). Breeder: Mr A. Sorger. Before leaving Germany, Lotte had been mated to Droll vom Kocher SchHIII (Sire: Lord von Birkenbuck SchHIII – Dam: Betty vom Kocher). The litter was born on 15 February 1955 and only one dog puppy survived, registered in the *Kennel Gazette* of September 1955 as Rintelna the Adjutant, subsequently exported to America.

Ajax and Lotte were mated and

produced Capt. Smith's 'B' litter, which was born on 11 July 1958. There were five males whose registration appears in December 1958 (Bandsman, Batman, Bombardier, Brigadier, Bugler). Four of the five puppies were sent to India and Pakistan, with only one male remaining in the UK. This was **Rintelna The Bombardier CDex, UDex,** owned by Mrs Mary MacPhail (Blackforest). Bombardier's son,
Champion Horst from Blackforest CDex (born 25 January 1966) is the only Show Champion with a Working Trial qualification. Horst's sons, Meister Maik CDex, UD (owned by Mary MacPhail) and Meister Mattais UDex (owned and trained by Mrs June Ockenden), carried on the working tradition. Bombardier was mated to a bitch called Chesara Portlaynum Bridgitte, which produced the breed's first Champion bitch – Ch. Chesara Dark Destiny, who was born on 10 June 1964.

Lotte was mated again to Ajax but only one bitch was to survive out of a litter of six. She was registered (*Kennel Gazette*, April 1960) as Rintelna the Chatelaine, born 20 September 1959, who left no progeny in this country, as she was taken to Australia with the Roy-Smith family in 1964.

A further breeding pair were imported in 1954 by Mrs Joanna Chadwick (Mallion) from Frau Marianne Bruns of the famous Eulenspiegel Kennel in Germany.

This pair had a great influence on the establishment of the breed in the UK.

Quinta Eulenspiegel of Mallion was born 28 February 1954 (*Sire: Asso von der Wakenitzburg SchH I – Dam: Blanka von Eppendorfer-Baum SchH III*), reported in the *Kennel Gazette* in August 1954. **Rudi Eulenspiegel of Mallion** was born on 21 May 1954 (*Sire: Quitto vom Landhaus – Dam: Flori Eulenspiegel SchH II*), according to the *Kennel Gazette* dated January 1955. Their first litter was born in February 1956 and was registered in June of that year. There were five males (Abelard of Mallion, also Adonis, Alaric, Alberichi, Ariel) and three females (Adda, Anne, Atlanta). Alaric was transferred to a Mr F. Brown and Adonis was later transferred to the ownership of Mrs Maud Wait. Abelard of Mallion was handled by Police Constable Roy Hunter. He was the first Rottweiler to serve in a police force and he was a really tough character who made some notable arrests.

Together, Rudi and Quinta produced several litters containing some very notable progeny. In the litter born 24 August 1957 – three females were registered, according to the *Kennel Gazette* December 1957 (Belinda of Mallion, also Brangane, Brunhilde) and four males (Balthasar, Boris, Brutus and Bruin). **Bruin of Mallion**, owned by Mrs Maud Wait

Bruin of Mallion CD, UDex, TDex: The first Rottweiler to become a Working Trials Champion.

(Lenlee), apart from being unbeaten in the show ring, became the breed's first Working Trials Champion gaining CDex, UDex and TDex titles in 1962. No Challenge Certificates were on offer then, but had there been, it is alleged he would have become a Show Champion. He did, however, gain entry into the Stud Book (No. 574AS).

Bruin's son, **Working Trials Champion Lenlee Gladiator**, owned and trained by Mrs S. Osborne, became the breed's second Working Trials Champion, eventually qualifying CDex, UDex, TDex and PDex. Gladiator was mated to Gamegards Border Tryst CDex (2 Reserve CCs), owned by Mrs Joyce Summers. This produced Nygra Night Watch, who produced two Show Champions (Ch. Graefin Tansy Baronin and Ch. Graefin Tamsley Witt) and an extremely successful Working Trials Champion, as well as other Championship show winners and

working trials qualified dogs.

Bruin's grandson, **Working Trials Champion Jacinto's Bolero** (*Sire: Nygra Night Watch – Dam: Gamegards Mellee*), qualified CDex, UDex, WDex, TDex and PDex, owned and handled by the late Terry Hadley, had great success in the 1970s and early 80s with Jake, who was an immensely powerful dog. He won four TD (Tracking Dog) Challenge Certificates in 1977, 1979, 1980 and 1981 and three PD (Police Dog) Certificates in 1977, 1978 (The Kennel Club Championship) and 1979.

Bruin of Mallion was a large dog, and so was Lenlee Gladiator – as indeed were many of the first working trial dogs. Remember, this breed was first and foremost a 'working' breed in its native country, so it is not surprising that the early dogs here did so well in working trials (which is the civilian equivalent of police work) and obedience. They had evolved from a long line of working/droving dogs, of substantial build and of correct construction.

Unfortunately, the Rottweiler in working trials has diminished somewhat in the UK over the years, possibly due to the requirement of the 6-foot-high scale jump, which requires the dog to land heavily on the other side of the jump, possibly damaging shoulders and elbows. However, properly trained dogs are taught to scale up one side then scale down the other side,

INFLUENTIAL ROTTWEILERS

Chesara Luther (later Ch.) born 22 February 1964 (*Sire: Dutch Ch. Baldur von Habenichts – Dam: Astrida*). Breeder: Mr. Meijerink. Imported from Holland by Judy and Larry Elsden (Chesara) this dog became the breed's first Champion.

Chesara Akilles (later Ch.) born 6 June 1966 (*Sire: International & Nordic Champion Fandangos Fairboy – Dam: Dackes Ina*). Breeder: Rolf Hamberg. Imported from Sweden, by the Elsdens.

Lars von der Hobertsberg (1968) (*Sire: Caro von Kuperdach SchHIII – Dam: Adda vom Dahl SchHIII*). Breeder: Frederich Berger.

Ch. Bulli von der Waldachquelle born 9 November 1970 (*Sire: International Champion Bulli von Hungerbuhl SchHII – Dam: Anka von Reichenbachle*). Both dogs imported from Germany by Mrs Joan Woodgate (now Blackmore) – Gamegards.

Castor of Intisari (later Ch.) born 5 December 1972 (*Sire: Int.Ch. Farro von het Brabantpark SchHII – Dam: Danish Ch. Ursula*). Imported from Denmark by Mr and Mrs Peter Radley – Intisari.

Ch. Chesara Dark Charles born 21 November 1979 (*Sire: Chesara Dark Herod – Dam: Chesara Juliette von Mark*). Bred by the Elsdens – Chesara. Top Stud Dog All Breeds 1983. A prolific stud dog behind many modern-day pedigrees.

Ch. Chesara Akilles.

Ch. Castor of Intisari.

Ch. Chesara Dark Charles.

rather than jumping straight off the top, when problems could occur. Several Rottweilers have competed successfully in working trials over the last 30 years and the sport is unique to the UK.

In partnership with Mrs Mary MacPhail, Capt. Roy-Smith brought in a bitch called **Vera vom Filstalstrand** (*Sire: Castor von Schussental – Dam: Bella vom Remstal*). Vera had been mated to one of the top German sires, Droll von der Brotzingergasse SchHII, prior to her arrival in the UK. Of the litter born on 2 December 1960, one of her sons, Rintelna the Dragoon, went on to become the first Australian Champion; the other son, Rintelna the Detective, went to the police; and her daughter, Anouk from Blackforest, was owned by Mary MacPhail.

THE 1960s/1970s

During the 1960s and 70s a sound breeding programme continued, which ensured the place of the Rottweiler as a popular pet and a prominent show dog. After World War II, the Kennel Club records just two Rottweilers being registered in the UK, but by 1964 this number had risen to 38. The 1960s saw many other imports and stud dogs making a significant impact on the development of the Rottweiler in the UK. Some would have a far-reaching effect on the breed. Some are listed on page 33, but many more can be found in books published purely for show and breeding enthusiasts.

With the popularity of the breed came the need to form a club, to ensure that the Rottweiler remained in sympathetic and knowledgeable hands. All owners were invited to attend a meeting following the judging at Crufts on 6 February 6 1960. From that initial meeting The Rottweiler Club was formed with Mrs Thelma Gray as its first President and Mrs Maud Wait as Secretary. The Chairman was Captain Frederick Roy-Smith MRCVS, and Mrs Mary Macphail was Treasurer. The Club met regularly and membership soon swelled to 700. They organised training sessions and shows and created a welfare scheme. Gradually, as interest in the breed grew, branches were established in other parts of the country, which eventually went on to become breed clubs in their own right.

Today, there are 10 Rottweiler breed clubs nationwide. Details of these clubs may be obtained from the Kennel Club. They are also listed in the Appendix.

RECENT YEARS

The Rottweiler was first registered by the British Kennel Club as a breed in its own right in 1965. It has been the 11th most popular breed for a number of years in the UK and registrations have risen steadily, from about 48 in 1966 to 6,575 in 2006. The Rottweiler had previously been little known to the general public until 1989, when the yearly registration was at an all-time high at 10,341 – a frighteningly high figure for such a small country. These are known as the 'dark days' when the breed hit the headlines in the newspapers, suffering the most appalling hysterics and persecution from the public and media alike. When

Champion Hanbar Nula, owned by Chris and Norma Window: A successful show dog in the UK.

Photo courtesy of Carol Ann Johnson.

there were a couple of attacks involving Pit Bull Terriers in the two years following, this resulted in the hastily-formed Dangerous Dogs Act 1991. There can be nobody in the UK who has not heard of the Rottweiler now. However, it is not within the remit of this book to outline the tragic incidents that caused the breed's notoriety.

Registrations for the first half of 2007 are at a modest 2,407, compared to the first half of 2006 when it was 3,099. However, not every Rottweiler puppy is registered, so the actual number is probably much higher. The yearly registered total is predicted to drop slightly now, due to the tail docking ban that came into force in the UK on 6 April 2007.

THE ROTTWEILER IN GERMANY

In Germany today the Rottweiler is the 10th most popular breed, with 1,528 registrations in 2006. Germany has some form of breed-specific legislation (BSL) in place, which consists of two lists of dog breeds. The first list contains breeds that are alleged to be dangerous, must not be bred from and must be muzzled.

The second list contains breeds that are considered to be dangerous unless they have passed a test proving that they are sociable dogs. The test consists of basic obedience, traffic awareness, and, most importantly, conversation (similar to the KC Good Citizen test, where the dog sits quietly while the owner is having a conversation) with the owner and

others, and, sometimes, inspection of the dog's home. After passing the test, these dogs can be kept by their owners with fewer restrictions. For example, the owners must have higher fences around their property than owners of other breeds, and dog handlers must have a minimum age or must prove knowledge in canine management. In addition these owners must pay extra dog taxes, which are sometimes 10 to 12 times higher than for a non-listed dog. Each community can declare its own tax rates. The Rottweiler is listed in this second category in four of the federal states of Germany. Of course, the ADRK is working very hard to overturn some of these laws and court restrictions.

The ADRK invented the ZTP (breed suitability test) to ensure that their breeding animals remained strong and healthy and of good temperament. Before a dog can take the ZTP he must have also obtained the BH [Begleithunde] (basic obedience test) and must be free of hip and elbow dysplasia. Some other countries followed this idea, and adapted these tests to suit their own needs. In Germany today, ADRK-registered dogs must still be subjected to these tests before they are used for breeding. Is it any wonder that German bloodlines are in demand all around the world?

THE ROTTWEILER IN AMERICA

The Rottweiler has flourished throughout the world and the breed is now well established in the United States. The first litter

German Champion Oxana vom Hause Neubrand: A typical specimen of the German Rottweiler.

Photo courtesy of vom Hause Neubrand kennel.

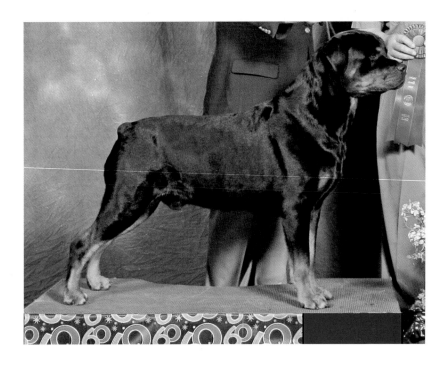

American Champion Ivoss Touch The Sun – No. 6 ranked Rottweiler in the United States, winning the Group at the Greater Miami Show in December 2007.

Photo courtesy of JAG Photography © 2007

bred there was in 1930 by a German emigrant, Otto Denny, who had already been an established breeder in his homeland. The 1930s were hard times and little progress was made for about 30 years. Following recognition by the American Kennel Club in 1931, the breed has risen to a most prominent position in the American show scene. In 1950 there were around 100 Rottweilers registered and the breed has risen in popularity since, so much so that, in the early 1990s, about 100,000 Rottweilers were being registered each year, making it the second most popular breed, behind the Labrador.

Unfortunately, this popularity resulted in dogs that were poorly bred and lacked socialisation, which culminated in unstable temperaments and bite incidents. Cities introduced various restrictions against the breed that took many responsible owners by surprise. Because the USA is such a vast country and comprised of many different states (which contain smaller counties, cities and smaller towns), each has its own laws. This means that, even within one county, there may be one city that restricts by breed and yet the city right next to it may not. Many owners were forced to get rid of their dogs, while some had to obtain liability insurance and muzzle their pets outside the home. Though breed-specific legislation is still creeping across America, owners are now challenging the unfair regulations and winning in courts of law. The American Rottweiler Club (ARC) and United States Rottweiler Club (USRC) are active in this fight.

Registrations in 2006 were up to 14,709, which made the Rottweiler the 17th most popular breed in the States. The ARC organise dog shows in a manner similar to the UK, but the USRC organise their shows along similar lines to the ADRK and they also arrrange Schutzhund-type trials. Generally, much more emphasis is placed on working/obedience and herding titles than in the UK.

THE ROTTWEILER TODAY

Today's Rottweiler remains a popular dog but is still very much over-bred with some puppies being sold at unjustifiably exorbitant prices.

Responsible breeding has restored the Rottweiler's fortunes in the US.

Photo courtesy of Grace Acosta – Acosta Rottweilers.

Some puppies are bred purely for monetary gain by those who have no real interest in our breed other than taking advantage of its popularity. This is not a good state of affairs. The rescue organisations are inundated with unwanted puppies, and adult dogs are dumped mercilessly each time there is a sensational news story involving dogs. Our Rottweilers are under an ever-present threat of being listed on the register of the Dangerous Dogs Act, which makes it a criminal offence to allow a dog to be dangerously out of control in a public place. Although no dog should ever be dangerously out of control in a public area, the restrictions put in force by the Dangerous Dogs Act are extremely limiting for dogs and

owners alike, and inclusion of the Rottweiler on this list will serve only to further damage the reputation of what is, in the right hands, a wonderful and loving companion dog. Of course, any dog can become aggressive under certain circumstances, but unlike breeds such as the Pit Bull, which were bred for their fighting abilities, the Rottweiler is not an inherently aggressive breed, and inclusion on the Dangerous Dogs Act is unnecesary and will only stigmatise the breed.

Fortunately for us, the instances of dangerous Rottweilers are very, very minimal. But we still have to be vigilant. Most Rottweilers enjoy their lives in the hands of sensible people who are prepared to protect the breed in every

possible way. It is essential to train good manners in the Rottweiler, which can be done by taking advantage of the Kennel Club's Good Citizen Dog Scheme (which teaches basic obedience and good manners). As classes teaching these skills are held up and down the country – there is no excuse not to participate. Ringcraft classes are also held and they will welcome a calm, obedient Rottweiler even if it is just to do some socialising rather than to be trained as a show dog.

The Rottweiler today is as reliable as he ever was in the right hands. Most are well trained and socialised, whether as show dogs, or for obedience, trials, police, therapy dogs, or as beloved family companions living out their lives happily in society.

A ROTTWEILER FOR YOUR LIFESTYLE

Chapter 3

Before you take on a Rottweiler, it is essential that you consider whether this breed is an appropriate choice for your lifestyle. In the right home, you will have a wonderful dog, but if you do not give your dog adequate attention, exercise or training, the experience can become deeply unpleasant for dog and owner alike. Therefore, it is essential that you think about a few basic considerations before making the commitment.

WORK COMMITMENTS

Most people have to go to work each day, so, if you are committed to a full-time job away from home, perhaps now is not the time to contemplate buying a Rottweiler. Likewise, if your lifestyle is such that the house is empty all day, it would be selfish to get a dog, particularly a breed

with such a thirst for activity as the Rottweiler, as he could become bored and damage things left lying around the house.

If you are a busy mother with several children to look after during the day, you may find you will not have sufficient time to properly care for and educate a young puppy or a wilful youngster, and this could result in the dog becoming untrained and wildly destructive. A good breeder would recommend that you wait until your children are older before taking on a Rottweiler, as it is such a huge commitment. If you live in cramped conditions with a very small garden, and have several children, then embarking on a Rottweiler – which will eventually grow into a large, boisterous animal – is not to be recommended either. Rottweilers need quality time and space.

Ideally, someone should be at

home with a new puppy, at least for a few weeks, during the initial training and settling-in period. Otherwise, there should be at least one person in the household who works close to home and is able to pop back regularly to let the dog out to relieve himself and to offer some much-needed attention. Once the dog is used to your routine and knows that you are coming back home eventually, this helps to stop any separation anxiety from forming.

Another option for working owners would be to employ a dog walker. This is someone who would have access to your home and call to take your dog out for a walk, either alone or with other dogs. A further service offered is that of the dog sitter, who would look after your dog in his/her own home while you are out at work. Some people offer their services in the local newspapers

A Rottweiler puppy is irresistible but also very demanding in terms of time and commitment.

but will also keep others out. At the same time, it will prevent the little fingers of inquisitive children from poking through and possibly getting nibbled.

Ideally, a garden large enough for the puppy to safely run around in will help to keep his muscles exercised and should prevent him from becoming bored. If you plan to keep your dog outside for most of the day, a small shed or kennel would be needed to protect the dog from hot sunshine or pouring rain. Also remember to provide a draught-proof bed and a heavy bucket of water that will not get tipped over. A word of warning if you are a keen gardener – leaving puppy alone outside for long periods will undoubtedly mean he will at some point present you with your recently planted shrub that he has dug up all by himself! So, if you can provide some form of stimulation, in the way of a large ball or toys, so much the better.

Inside the house, you must ensure that the puppy cannot climb the stairs, as the last thing you want is a puppy falling and breaking his bones. A puppy/child gate is a most useful item for this purpose. A puppy gate can also be used in the kitchen area, ensuring that the puppy can be left in safety and peace while eating. This is important especially if there are other animals or children in the house. Smooth, shiny laminate floors are not ideal for a new puppy, as he will be unable to gain a grip on the surface and this

or can even be recommended by doggy friends. There are national pet-sitting organisations that use only registered and insured people, so that you can be assured of a trustworthy, reliable sitter. It would be a good idea to make sure you and your puppy are properly bonded to each other before you try these options.

Other than that, you may have to rely on a friend or a neighbour who could let your dog out during the day. However, bear in mind that, if this becomes a long-term, regular arrangement, you may be testing the limits of your friendship…

HOME AND GARDEN
A safe, secure back garden with a six-foot-high, dog-proof fence is a *must* before you contemplate getting any large dog. Fencing will not only keep your dog in

COUNTING THE COST

Most pedigree dogs will have Champions in their lineage, but this alone will not necessarily guarantee health, temperament, or a quality dog. The breeder and the breeding are the important factors.

Most good breeders have spent many years and lots of heartache getting to where they are now in order to produce a good-quality, healthy animal with a sound temperament. If you go to a reputable breeder, you are far more likely to get your money's worth. The average cost of a puppy should be about £600 to £800 (based on 2007 prices), but you can pay a lot more for a show-quality animal from some of the top bloodlines (between £800 to £1,000, for example). You really don't want to pay less than around £300, or buy anything from the Friday Ads for £200! If you do, and then you find out the puppy has health or behavioural problems, don't be surprised. As with everything else in life, you get what you pay for, but don't get ripped off at either end of the money scale.

It is vital that you do your research by speaking to several breeders. Use the internet; sound out a few breeders by phone and see what their attitude is. If they offer you a puppy there and then without asking you any questions, leave them well alone and try elsewhere. You should expect to be thoroughly questioned by a reputable Rottweiler breeder.

Once you have purchased your puppy, you may want to think about insurance, as veterinary fees can be expensive, particularly for the large breeds. There are not many large breeds that can go through life without a visit or two to the vet. Yearly vaccinations and flea and worming medications also have to be accounted for on a regular basis and these are the very least expenses you should be prepared to pay for. Also remember: the bigger the dog, the bigger the veterinary bills.

Should you wish to take your pet abroad, he will have to undertake a course of rabies vaccinations. If your pet stays at home while you are away, then kennelling fees will have to be counted as well.

Whether you wish to feed a natural diet (raw meat, raw bones, vegetables, rice etc.) or a ready-made complete diet, there are many brands of dog diets on display in the pet shop. However, you should be guided by your breeder when you collect your puppy. (A word of warning here: many vets sell dog food – which is vastly expensive.) Depending on the size, age, sex and activity level of your dog, he will probably eat between 3kg and 4kg of a good brand of dog food a week. This would generally be between 400g and 500g of dry food divided into two meals a day. This kind of dog food costs between £20 and £35 for a 15kg bag for a good-quality mix.

Your Rottweiler will appreciate a garden that is large enough to allow free-running exercise.

is not good for his hips. A piece of carpeting would be a good idea until the puppy is large enough to gain a good foothold. Also ensure that your new puppy cannot get access to electrical wires and sockets, for obvious reasons.

TIME
As a bare minimum, you really should spend an hour or so each day playing with your Rottweiler puppy and teaching him games and training exercises to stimulate his mind. You also need to think about the time involved in grooming and checking over the important parts regularly (ears for

wax or canker; eyes and nose for discharge; that the baby teeth are coming out and not impacting on the adult teeth which are coming through; checking genitals for signs of discharge; trimming the nails to ensure they are kept short, etc.). This not only applies to puppies, but must also continue into the dog's adult life. If you only have one dog to worry about, this may not be too much time to set aside, but what if you already have other dogs or pets in the household? They all need attention and quality time while you are trying to integrate a new puppy into the household regime,

and you must bear this all in mind before you buy.

HOLIDAYS
It is an unfortunate fact that much holiday accommodation in the UK will not accept dogs, so you may have to rely on boarding kennels. Seek out kennels that are Rottweiler-friendly, as some are not, possibly due to negative publicity. It is as well to book a boarding kennel very early on in your holiday plans, as the popular ones get booked up very quickly, particularly during the school holidays. Ask questions first, then go and see the kennels for yourself

It is a great bonus if you can take your Rottweiler on holiday with you.

before you make the commitment. Make sure you are happy with the cleanliness and the amount of contact each animal gets. Some kennels will walk dogs (on leads) and some will not, although each animal should have its own concrete run attached to the kennel. Some kennels may not welcome visitors and these are the ones to avoid. A caring, friendly boarding kennel will welcome inspections by prospective clients. Boarding rates are usually per dog, per day, including VAT and insurance. However, this would depend on the area in which you live, as prices vary. Remember, an up-to-date vaccination certificate is required by all boarding kennels.

Sometimes it may be cheaper, or more convenient, to employ the services of a friend or make enquiries about home-boarding or dog-sitting services. Some sitters take up residence in your home while you are away, so that your dogs are kept to their normal walking and feeding routine. This is much better for them and for your peace of mind. Sitters will be highly experienced people (or they should be, especially if they are sitting for a house full of Rottweilers). There are many house-sitting agencies on the market and these can found by accessing the internet or the local newspaper. Your vet may also have recommendations. The agency will discuss your pet's routine and also your preferences for a sitter, e.g. male/female/couple, with own car. All home-sitters are non-smokers, without accompanying pets. The best services are offered nationwide and you can set off on your trip secure in the knowledge that your home, possessions and pets are being carefully looked after while you are away. Ensure you are thoroughly bonded with your pet before you try these options.

YOUR ROTTWEILER COMPANION

If you want a large, loyal, easy-to-care-for companion as a pet, a Rottweiler would be your ideal choice. The Rottweiler is very easy to live with and does not demand constant attention, like some of the smaller breeds. He will always follow you from room to room, wanting to be near you, but he is just as content to lie quietly at your feet. However, mention the words 'walk' or 'ball' and he will immediately spring into action. He is generally not vocal or yappy, until a stranger walks up to the house – then he will let you know!

If you are looking for a Rottweiler to show, the best place to start is at a dog show. Find out which particular bloodlines appeal to you, as within each breed there is a variation of type. If you decide you might like to have a go, enrol at show-training classes and start your show career at a local companion dog show to see if you like it, and whether you have the basic show skills. If you do, then you could advance on to the Open show circuit, which is more competitive and demanding. If you gain some success there, you will probably get bitten by the bug and will want to advance on to the Championship shows, which are held most summer weekends up and down the country. Exhibiting dogs costs money and to be at the very top is a serious business where the competition can be very intense – so you will have to develop a thick skin and have deep pockets.

A Rottweiler will bring fun and joy into your life.

It is essential that all breeding stock is health checked to reduce the risk of inherited disease.

FINDING A BREEDER

The Kennel Club should be your first port of call for a reputable breeder. The Kennel Club will direct you to an authorised breed club for your area, who will be able to tell you which of their club members may have a litter available now or in the near future. The members of most Rottweiler breed clubs are bound by a breeding code of ethics and they will ensure that their breeding animals are of good temperament. They will also ensure that the usual health checks (hip and elbow X-raying and heart testing) will have been carried out before a mating takes place. Most of these breeders are known as 'hobby breeders' and

their breeding animals are their day-to-day companions. By going through a breed club in this way, you are ensuring that you not only benefit from their valuable experience and knowledge of perhaps 20-plus years, but also you will receive a great back-up and after-sales service, plus a contract – which is the very least you should expect from a breeder and which is not available from someone selling dogs through the classifieds in your local newspaper.

The Kennel Club will also be able to supply you with details of breeders on its Accredited Breeder Scheme. These breeders must adhere to a strict code of ethics and health schemes, laid

down by the Kennel Club before they are admitted to the scheme. Their breeding animals will have had breed-specific tests carried out. The Rottweiler breed clubs have stipulated what is a usable breed mean score, meaning that puppies bred by accredited breeders following breed club guidelines, will be as physically sound and healthy as possible. Furthermore, an accredited breeder will have permanently identified their breeding animals by DNA, microchip or tattoo; the puppies will have been whelped and reared in accordance with good practice and adequately socialised with human contact; and the breeder will provide a record of the

A specialist breeder may only have one or two litters a year.

vaccinations of the puppy and provide a clearly laid out contract of sale. The contract will also explain if any Kennel Club restrictions have been placed on the puppies,

The Kennel Club permits the use of two endorsements on litter registrations – Progeny Not Eligible for Registration and Export Pedigree Not Allowed. Neither of these endorsements prevents the dog from being bred from or sent abroad, but does prevent any litters being registered with the Kennel Club and the dog from being registered by an overseas kennel club. All endorsements are placed by the breeder at the time of registration of the litter. The use of Kennel Club

endorsements is undoubtedly beneficial to breeders as a safeguard to protect animals which have been carefully and responsibly bred. As certain breeds are known to suffer from particular health problems, the breeder may wish that any animals bred by them are examined under the official health schemes prior to being bred from. To avoid disputes the Kennel Club strongly advises that all breeders draw up a private contract when selling puppies. If endorsements are being used, the contract should mention why these have been placed and under what circumstances (if any) they would be removed. The contract should be signed and dated by both purchaser and

vendor, showing that both have agreed to the terms.

Be sure to search carefully for a responsible and knowledgeable breeder who places high priority on breeding for good health and sound temperament. Such a breeder will interrogate and educate potential buyers carefully, and will continue to be available for advice and consultation whenever needed. A good breeder will sell a puppy with a contract and will usually insist on receiving the dog back if you are unable to keep him for whatever reason. Remember, the Rottweiler is a strong and powerful breed and owning one is a huge responsibility. A puppy is a blank sheet of paper – what you put there is up to you.

CHOOSING A HEALTHY PUPPY

Unfortunately, most breeds these days suffer from one or more inherited defects and/or health problems and the Rottweiler is no exception. The most common health problems with Rottweilers include:

- Hip dysplasia
- Elbow dysplasia/ osteochondritis dessicans
- Cruciate ligament rupture
- Heart problems
- Entropion.

(For more information on these conditions, see Chapter 8.)

Responsible breeding practices have drastically reduced the instances of these problems in the Rottweiler over the last 15 years or so. Most responsible breeders will have had their breeding animals regularly health-checked and will also take part in specific health schemes organised by the British Veterinary Association (BVA) and the Kennel Club, such as X-raying for hip and elbow dysplasia and checking the heart. These diseases have a strong genetic disposition and therefore screening of dogs' hips and elbows by X-rays helps breeders to select the most suitable dogs for breeding.

When a dog is screened for hip or elbow dysplasia, X-rays are taken of the animal's joints and are then forwarded to the British Veterinary Association for 'scoring'. In both of these scoring systems, each dog is identified either by microchip or tattoo, to ensure the correct dog is being offered for X-ray. The X-rays for each dog may only be submitted to the BVA for scoring once in the dog's lifetime. The owner receives a copy of the score sheet, which shows the status of the bones. You should ask to see copies of the various certificates for heart, hips and elbows of the parents of your puppy; if the breeder doesn't show you these certificates, or doesn't have them – go elsewhere for your puppy

It is worth mentioning here that if you plan to do agility or working trials (where there is considerable jumping involved), it is essential that you seek out animals from sound breeding.

HIP DYSPLASIA

The hip-scoring system warrants explanation, as it is quite confusing for the uninitiated. The score is determined by allocating points to each imperfection on the ball and socket of each hip joint. The minimum (best) score for each hip is 0, while the maximum (worst) is 53, making a total of 106 when multiplied by two for both hips. Basically: the higher the score, the more likelihood there is of hip dysplasia developing.

The hip scores should be well within the average (mean) score for the breed, which, currently, is 13 for the Rottweiler. The BVA advises that breeders wishing to control HD should breed only from animals with hip scores below the breed mean score. So, if the parents of your puppy have scores below 13, then that increases the chances of your puppy having sound hips. If the parents had a score of 0:0 then that would be perfect scores! You should look for scores as even as possible, e.g. you don't want an uneven 1:12, as this could indicate a problem in one hip. If possible, try to ascertain the scores of the ancestors of the puppy's parents. Some breeders note these on the animal's pedigree.

HEART TESTING

Some breeders are now heart testing their breeding animals through the BVA scheme. This is a quick and painless test done by a qualified cardiologist vet. Electrodes are attached to the dog's skin and a paper read-out is produced (just the same as a human's heart test). A certificate is given to the owner, stating whether the heart was normal or abnormal, and only those animals who receive a normal reading should be bred from.

HOME-REARED OR KENNEL-REARED?

Preferably get your Rottweiler from an established 'hobby breeder' or a show kennel. Do not choose a commercial kennel where there may be several breeds on offer. The dedicated

ELBOW DYSPLASIA

Elbow dysplasia (ED) is a common condition manifesting as a variety of developmental disorders within the dog's elbow. It can lead to osteoarthritis of the elbow joint(s). The scoring system is totally different from the hip scoring system, and can be quite baffling. The grades for each elbow are not added together as they are for the two hips in the hip dysplasia scheme.

The overall grade given for both elbows is the grade that was given to the elbow with the highest score. The lower the grade, the less the degree of elbow dysplasia evident on the X-ray. The BVA recommends that breeders wishing to reduce the risk of elbow dysplasia should select their breeding animals only from dogs and bitches with overall elbow grades of 0 or 1.

Two X-rays are taken of each elbow and the grading system is simple:

Grade	Description
0	Normal
1	Mild ED
2	Moderate ED or a primary lesion
3	Severe ED

hobby breeder/show kennel will probably have one or two litters a year only, and will almost certainly have a special place in the house where the puppies are born. These puppies are fortunate and will have constant daily household noise and handling from the breeder and others in the house, which benefits the socialising process greatly. Once the puppies are ready to be weaned and are up on their feet, running around, that is the time when breeders will usually put them into an outside kennel. Some breeders even play a CD of loud noises, fireworks, babies crying and day-to-day noises in order to accustom the puppies to the outside world.

MEET THE FAMILY

You should always see a puppy with its mother wherever you purchase your puppy from and this is the very least you should expect. However, you may not see the father, as he will probably be owned by another breeder. However, if you are interested, your breeder will tell you where

he can be seen. Few experienced breeders use their own stud dog (unless he is an imported animal of outstanding quality), preferring to drive many hundreds of miles, or even go abroad, to use the best stud dog for their breeding bitch, which will probably be unrelated.

Pay particular attention to the temperament of the parents of your puppy, as this is a good guide to the future temperament of the puppy.

Depending on when you are allowed to view a litter, you may also see related dogs. Most

breeders will probably have a relative of the puppy in their home, either an aunt or a cousin, and will be only too happy to allow you to meet them. Some breeders may mate close family members (e.g. grandfather to granddaughter or cousin to cousin), but be wary of puppies produced by mating father to daughter or mother to son. Definitely avoid a puppy produced through a brother to sister match, as this is a 'no, no' and would probably not be registered with the Kennel Club.

You will want to see the mother with her puppies, as this will give you some idea of the temperament they are likely to inherit.

VIEWING THE LITTER

Most good breeders will welcome puppy buyers quite early on in the development of a litter, as this helps towards socialisation. Generally, the best time to view puppies is when they are being weaned and they are up on their legs, running about, at around four to five weeks. Their characters will have begun to develop and they are much more interesting to watch. Some breeders identify each puppy by a coloured collar, or mark them in some way (e.g. Tippex). Most puppies are ready to go their new homes at around seven to eight weeks of age and certainly not at six weeks or younger.

If you visit a breeder's premises or a commercial kennels, be absolutely sure that you have the strength of character to walk away if you are not happy. Some really successful kennels may have both parents of a litter, but, in general, if there are both parents, this can be an indication of a puppy farm or backyard breeder and you should be very careful.

Irresponsible breeders rely on the soft-touch buyer, and will keep breeding over and over again, and usually many times from one bitch. There is nothing more difficult than walking away from a cuddly, fluffy teddy bear, so be prepared.

WHAT TO LOOK FOR

If you are looking for a companion or pet puppy, your requirements are simple – good temperament and a sound, healthy animal. If you are looking for a puppy to show, your requirements are much more stringent.

For any puppy, first and foremost you should look for a bright-eyed, happy puppy, not one who is skulking at the back of a kennel or who will not come forward happily to meet you. The puppy should not appear lethargic, or have mucous coming from its eyes or nose. Neither should the puppy be extremely pot-bellied, as this could indicate a severe case of worms. Also, check for hernias (a lump around the puppy's belly-button or in the groin area). If there is a lump there, do not choose that puppy or ask for a reduction in the cost, as the puppy may possibly need surgery in later life.

When choosing a show puppy, look for a head that appears quite blocky, not narrow or pinched, with a skull that is not domed; smallish, neat ears not too low down on the skull; dark blue eyes (which will become dark brown, as the puppy grows); and tight eye rims, as you don't want the skin around the eyes to be very loose, showing the insides of the eye rims. Neither do you want the puppy to have lots of wrinkles and excess skin on its head, as this generally does not improve and could develop into an eye problem called entropion.

Ask the breeder to show you

The breeder will 'stand up' each puppy and help you to assess show potential.

the puppy's teeth. These should be strong and evenly placed in the mouth, with the upper jaw just overlapping the lower jaw and the teeth slightly touching, in what is called a 'scissor' bite. If either the top jaw or the bottom jaw jut out considerably and there is a wide gap between the teeth of the upper and lower jaws, the puppy is possibly overshot or undershot. This is not correct and the puppy should not be sold as a show-quality puppy. Bear in mind that a puppy's jaws and bone structure are going through many growth changes during the first months of life.

The puppy should have a firm, cobby body and good bone structure, which should appear strong and in proportion to the puppy, giving good angulation front and rear (the angle of limbs to body – see Chapter 7 for more information). The puppy should be able to get up and run about without obvious effort.

The puppy's feet should be rather cat-like, not long and flat. When viewed from the front the legs should be as straight as possible, with the feet not turning in or out. The coat of an eight-week-old puppy will probably be a bit fluffy still, but you should be able to see some harsher hairs coming through, which will indicate a correct adult coat in later life. Of course, there should not be a solid patch of white hairs on the chest of a prospective show puppy, although a few wispy white hairs on the chest will almost certainly disappear.

Unfortunately, most first-time owners expect to get the pick of the litter, but this is rarely the case. Most serious breeders put themselves first because they want a puppy for showing or breeding a couple of years down the line. They will obviously keep the best. Once the breeder has made their choice, the surplus puppies are the ones that will be on sale for you. Usually it is the breeder who will decide which will be the right puppy for you, because of your family lifestyle, whether you have children, elderly people, other pets in the household, etc. A good breeder will try to match the temperament of the puppy to his new home environment.

Some breeders use a method of classifying the temperament of their puppies. This is called 'puppy testing'. It is usually carried out by somebody who has studied canine behaviour and who knows what they are doing. This testing is always carried out at exactly seven weeks (49 days old), as it is believed that the neural pathways in the brain have fully developed by this time. The tests are simple and reveal the puppy's true character (before they go to their new homes and have new experiences imprinted on their minds). Not all puppies will have the same test results, and the differences will assist in placing the puppy in the most appropriate environment.

The aim is to find a healthy puppy that is typical of the breed.

Sometimes a breeder may have an adult Rottweiler who needs rehoming.

BOOKING YOUR PUPPY

Most dedicated breeders will have taken bookings for their puppies for months (sometimes up to two years) before the litter is even born. The average litter size for Rottweilers is generally between six and 10; but there have been disappointing disasters with as little as two or none. So always try to have a contingency plan. To avoid disappointment you should do your homework and visit several breeders before placing an order for a puppy. Choose one breeder you like and stick with them. Do not place an order for a puppy with several breeders, as word will soon get around and you may not get one at all! Tell the breeder your intentions for the puppy on the first phone call, i.e. whether it is to be a replacement for a cherished family companion, or whether you want to do some form of obedience work or exhibiting in the show ring. This can have a bearing on the puppy the breeder will choose for you.

CHOOSING AN ADULT DOG

If you prefer not to go through the time-absorbing period of having to educate and house-train a very young puppy, you might consider getting an older puppy or young adult, perhaps around six to nine months old. Sometimes breeders 'run on' puppies, keeping back one or two puppies that they feel are potentially show quality. The breeder will want to watch the puppies grow and will pay particular attention to their teeth and jaws, which have to be perfect for exhibiting. It is sometimes worth contacting several breeders to find out if they have such a puppy or a young adult, which has perhaps not come up to the mark for the show ring and which the breeder is prepared to sell.

Again, the choice of animal

would have to fit in with your particular lifestyle. If you are young at heart then a dog with bounding energy will probably suit you; but if you are of slower years then perhaps a quieter, more 'ploddy' dog would be better for you. You should visit the breeder several times to make sure you have chosen the right dog and will not have to return the dog, which would be upsetting both for the dog and for you.

CHOOSING A RESCUED DOG

If you would rather not go through the time-consuming regime of training and rearing a puppy, or if you simply prefer to have a more mature dog, you may consider homing a rescued dog. There are two Rottweiler welfare schemes organised by experienced Rottweiler people – Rottweiler Welfare Association and Rottweilers in Need (see Appendix, page 148), although there are other places where you can obtain a Rottweiler. You should expect to be thoroughly vetted by any organisation offering you a rescued dog, to ensure you are capable of owning a Rottweiler; they may also visit your home. Not all dogs in rescue are strays; they can be there for a variety of reasons. Some will have been handed in perhaps because of the owner's inability to handle a large dog with a challenging temperament – or some may be the result of a family break-up or bereavement. Some were bought on a whim

and then abandoned when they suddenly grew out of puppyhood. Rescued dogs may also have been abused or neglected and may suffer behavioural problems as a result. On the other hand, they are often well-behaved, loving animals that only need care and affection and

who end up in rescue through no fault of their own. Taking on a rescued Rottweiler can be quite challenging – you must be prepared to put in a lot of hard work. The rescue organisation may be able to supply you with the animal's history, but this is not always the case.

Taking on a rescued dog is hard work – but it can be very rewarding.

THE NEW ARRIVAL

Chapter 4

T he key to successfully integrating your Rottweiler with your family and lifestyle is to make sure you prepare well in advance.

DOG-PROOFING

Make your home as dog-friendly as possible. Not only will this help to ensure your Rottweiler's safety, but it will also allow you to relax more, knowing your dog cannot cause too much damage to either himself or your property, therefore enabling you to enjoy the experience of owning a dog that much more.

Firstly, decide in advance where the dog will sleep. Preferably this will be in an enclosed area – the kitchen or utility room is ideal. The bed should be in a dry, comfortable position. Dogs like to lie in a corner, out of the way.

Give some thought to areas of the house that you want to

There is lot of work to be done before your Rottweiler puppy arrives in his new home.

55

remain off-limits to your Rottweiler. Most owners are happy to allow their dog the run of the garden and either the kitchen or utility room. However, they may not want to allow access to the whole house. If you have ever seen a boisterous Rottweiler charge into the house from a wet and muddy garden, you will understand. You might also want to use a baby/stair gate in the early stages, to teach your dog that he is not allowed upstairs. Allowing a dog to be 'above' you, such as when you are going upstairs and he is already at the top – can cause problems. Your Rottweiler may challenge you and not allow you to come up. As a Rottweiler goes through stages of development, there is an increasing possibility that he will test his dominance with you. The inexperienced owner will find this extremely problematic, so don't let it happen. Consider the house rules in advance and be consistent. Allowing your dog on your bed may be cute to begin with, but when you then tell him to get off and he

growls, you have a problem that you have created.

In areas where your Rottweiler will be allowed, try to make the area as safe as possible. Puppies and young dogs will chew, so make sure there are no electric plugs or cables around. Basically, if something can be picked up and chewed, then move it. A good way of making sure you have dog-proofed as much as possible is to get down on hands and knees and crawl around the room. This will allow you to see things from your dog's perspective.

EQUIPMENT

BEDDING
Don't waste lots of money on fancy bedding, as all your dog needs is something comfortable and dry. Remember, whatever bedding you choose will have to be cleaned from time to time, especially if your dog arrives in the wet winter months. If you have taken on a rescue dog, the bedding might get shredded over the first few days if the dog has any anxiety problems. If you have a puppy or a juvenile dog, he will grow very quickly, and a small bed, no matter how well-made, will soon be outgrown and need replacing.

FOOD AND WATER
You will normally be given a small supply of food by the breeder, when you collect the new dog or puppy, but it is a good idea to find out in advance what food your new Rottweiler is used to and get a supply beforehand. If you must change his diet, do not do so until your dog has settled in.

A puppy will be happy to settle on some cosy bedding.

You will need two bowls – one for food and one for water. Ideally, the feeding bowl should be stainless steel, so that it can be easily cleaned. The water bowl will need to be large. Rottweilers love to put their head right into the bucket, and dogs need lots of water, particularly in hot weather.

COLLAR AND LEAD

Depending on the size of your dog, have an appropriate collar and lead. Please don't buy a thick, leather buckled collar, especially one with studs on. They are useless for training and they give a bad impression of the breed. Neither should you use a harness, as it is nothing more than a device to teach your dog to pull. You want your Rottweiler to walk calmly and obediently beside you, not drag you as a Husky drags a sled. A soft, nylon or buckle-type collar is suitable for a juvenile or adult, but a lightweight, nylon collar is better for a puppy. The size of lead will vary depending on

the age of the dog, but for a juvenile or adult, it should be strong leather (not nylon) and fairly wide. A thin nylon lead will cut into your hand if the dog pulls. Conversely, please don't use a chain lead, as this will also hurt your hands and gives a wrong impression of the breed; also a heavy lead will be far too much weight on a puppy's neck. For this first couple of years of your Rottweiler's life, you will need two or three leads, of different sizes.

Do not forget that, by law, dogs need to have an identification

disc attached to the collar when they are in a public place. This should be engraved with your name and contact details. (It is not essential to have the dog's name on the disc, although most owners do.) Microchipping is becoming universally acceptable, and is a quick and relatively simple process, carried out by a vet or a suitably trained person. A small 'chip', shaped like a grain of rice, is injected beneath the skin, usually in the area of the back of the neck, between the shoulders. The chip holds a unique identifying number, which is recorded on a national database, together with details of the dog and the owner. Dog wardens and vets carry microchip scanners, which can read the details of the chip and return the dog if he becomes lost.

CRATES

A cage or crate can help a dog to feel secure. It is certainly useful when a dog needs to be isolated, perhaps when injured or ill, and certainly during initial training. A crate can be used when rehoming an older or adult

It will not be long before your puppy looks on his crate as his own special den.

TOYS

A puppy will go through a chewing phase, so make sure you provide safe toys for him.

Toys must be safe and too big to be swallowed. Don't buy flimsy toys. A Rottweiler will soon tear them to shreds with his tremendously powerful jaws. The Kong is a good toy, as it is made of very hard rubber, which will withstand all but the most determined Rottweiler. Being beehive shaped, Kongs bounce in different directions when dropped and puppies love this. They also have a hole in the middle and this is an ideal place to stuff food. The dog will soon work out the food is there, and, by experimenting, will eventually find a way to get the food out. A Kong is also useful when leaving the dog alone for the first few nights. Stuff it with something tasty and smelly, and it will occupy him all night!

Don't spend a fortune on fancy toys. In particularly, do not buy cheap, thin plastic squeaky toys, as Rottweiler puppies chew bits off and these can get swallowed. There are toys

dog, as it provides somewhere to lie safely while the dog becomes used to his new environment. It is also somewhere to keep him out of mischief and to prevent him from chewing everything in sight. Also, as you gradually build up his time spent alone it will help the dog get used to your absences and reduce separation anxiety. If you have more than one dog, it is often best to confine the new dog,

particularly overnight, in the early stages.

There are many sturdy, collapsible mesh cages on the market, and one of these is probably best. You can see if the dog is happy in the cage and you can either close the entrance or leave it open. Otherwise, you can quickly fold it up and put it away until needed. As Rottweiler puppies grow at an alarming rate, make sure you get the largest cage you

can accommodate. As a rough guide, a five-month-old puppy will be around the same size as a Border Collie, an eight- or nine-month-old pup can be nearly twice that size.

FINDING A VET
Before you collect your dog, seek out a good veterinary practice that is Rottweiler-friendly (as some are afraid of the breed). Ask if you can take your dog along to just say

called "raggers" which puppies love to chew, as they help pull out the baby teeth, but don't get involved in tug of war games, which could lead to growling and conflict. Give an empty plastic bottle to a dog and he will play with it for hours. Dogs are like children – they often ignore the contents and prefer to play with the packaging. When the dog's teeth eventually burst the bottle, find another – absolutely free! Word of warning: the small ring of plastic that is left on the neck of the bottle when the seal is broken is fascinating to a Rottweiler. He will spend ages trying to get it off – when he does, take it away, as it may get swallowed.

Some other ideas for toys for puppies include a stuffed sock; plastic flowerpot; a worn piece of cloth; or an old glove – but don't use old shoes for obvious reasons! The object is to keep the dog amused and to exercise the teeth of a puppy. As long as the dog is happy, why spend money on expensive toys?

A rubber kong will help to keep your Rottweiler occupied.

'hello'. A good vet should agree to this. Your new puppy or dog can then meet the vet and nurses, have a fair amount of attention and leave happily, without any memories of probing fingers or needle-induced pain that might affect his future attitude to the vet. Organise another visit fairly soon afterwards for vaccination and routine worming or flea control.

Some breeders do not vaccinate their puppies, as vets have different regimes in different parts of the country and it is better to start from fresh. Remember: until fully vaccinated, a puppy is vulnerable and should not be allowed to walk outside your property, so do not take him out until your vet gives the all clear. A rescue dog may or may not have been vaccinated and you must clarify this when you collect him.

COLLECTING YOUR ROTTWEILER

Whether you are collecting a puppy or a rescue dog, make sure you collect all of the relevant paperwork: contract, bill of sale, pedigree, any vaccination certificates, and diet advice. A good breeder will give you a small piece of the puppy's bedding, as it will have the puppy's smell on it and will help him to settle in his new surroundings.

At last the big day comes, and it is time to collect your puppy.

Plan to collect the dog as early in the day as possible, so that he has plenty of time to settle in when you get back home. You certainly don't want to get home late at night and then expect the dog to go to bed immediately in a house he is not familiar with.

Depending on the length of the journey, a young puppy may feel more secure riding on your lap, but an older dog should be contained. You will either need a cage in the car, or, if you have a hatchback or estate, some barrier to separate the dog from the front of the car. A dog tends to feel more secure if he is contained. Break your journey, especially in the case of a puppy. First experiences last, even with animals, so don't leave your puppy with the memory of hours upon hours of travel and discomfort. You may then have a dog that dreads car travel forever.

Another word of warning: if your puppy whines or barks during his first journey in the car – ignore it, because if you say "it's okay, good boy" the puppy will assume you mean it is okay to whine and bark in the car!

Take the puppy into the garden as soon as you get home; let him explore and be prepared to wait for him to relieve himself – have your treats ready and immediately make a fuss of him and give him a treat when he does.

The training has started and so too has the bonding. If you have collected a juvenile or older dog,

Unless you are extremely fortunate, you will probably have some distance to travel home, so be prepared. Ask the breeder not to feed the puppy before the journey – a puppy will probably have no experience of car travel, so there is a fair chance he will be sick. A rescue dog may or may not be used to car travel, so make sure you ask in advance. Don't wear your best clothes, as it is likely that, by the time you arrive home, they will not be in pristine condition. Take paper towels, an old blanket and plenty of newspaper, wet wipes (for you), together with a bin bag to put any soiled items into. Hopefully, you will not need these, but it is better to be prepared than suffer a smelly car on your first journey together. There should ideally be two people to collect a puppy – one to drive and one to see to the dog.

then now is the time to take him to your regular walking area. Don't forget to take a 'poo bag' with you, to clear up any mess along the way.

THE FIRST NIGHT

The first night can be quite difficult, particularly with a young puppy separated from his littermates for the first time. Expect cries of anguish to tear your heart strings – but do not weaken. The best thing to do is to make sure the puppy has been fed, exercised and given the chance to relieve himself and explore his new home. Make sure there is nothing around to hurt him. Take him to his warm bed and leave him. If you are leaving him in a crate, it is a good idea to cover it with a blanket. Turn the lights off and go. If you are a light sleeper, or inclined to be over sympathetic, take a couple of earplugs – and use them! Some puppies will adapt almost immediately and settle down, yet some can take several days. Resist all temptation to sympathise with the dog in the night, and above all, do not take him to your bedroom. If you give in each time the puppy whines and barks for attention, he has won the day and he is in "control".

A rescued dog will almost certainly have been used to sleeping alone and may well find the first night a little easier. Use the crate and leave your new Rottweiler with a few toys and warm blankets. These should see him happily through the first night. Don't leave a water bowl, as it will get tipped over and soak the bedding.

THE WIDER WORLD

You must introduce the new arrival to any other family members as soon as possible. However, do this in a thoughtful way to ensure the adjustment is as smooth as possible.

Taking on a rescued dog can be a very rewarding challenge. Rescue organisations will not rehome dogs that are dangerous, and most rescued dogs need new homes through no fault of their own – the previous owners separated, the dog grew too big, a new baby came along, etc. Whatever the reason, the dog may have a few problems and you should try to establish what these are before you consider taking on the dog. Be aware that some rescued dogs may not have received adequate socialisation with other dogs or people.

Your puppy will feel lonely and bewildered the first night he spends away from his littermates.

If you take on a rescued dog, you will need to be very sensitive to his needs while he settles in.

MEETING THE FAMILY

Introducing the newcomer to adults and children is extremely important and you will find that a number of friends will want to drop in, especially if they have children. Give yourselves time to bond first. Puppies and children both like to play, but care must be taken that the children are not too boisterous. An apprehensive dog or puppy does not need half a dozen screaming kids frightening him to death. Puppies will naturally 'mouth' (see Chapter 1), and, with teeth like needles, they will easily draw blood. Supervised play is fine, but mouthing must not be allowed.

Do not allow anyone to stick his or her fingers in the puppy's mouth. Some people seem to have a fascination for this. They allow the puppy to chew their fingers and even encourage it. Explain politely but firmly that they are teaching the dog to bite, and that in a few months' time it will not be as funny. How can you tell a dog one minute that it is okay to chew fingers, but some months later punish him for doing so? Consistency is vital. The same applies to your own family members. The dog needs affection and training, but most important is consistency. Everyone must contribute to the training and the most important factor is to choose a set of commands that will be used by everyone. It is no good you telling the dog to "Wait" when others tell him to "Stay". This will only confuse the dog.

The family should meet an older dog in a calm, friendly way. The dog should be handled and given a few titbits, then allowed to either mingle or to find a corner as he wishes. He should be given the opportunity to explore. If the newcomer is male – and particularly if you have any other male dogs in the house – you must anticipate that he will probably 'cock his leg'. This is unfortunately a natural trait (he is advertising his presence) but you have to stop this behaviour as soon as possible. Gradually, the dog should become confident and comfortable in his new surroundings and react happily with everyone.

LIVING WITH OTHER DOGS

If you already have another dog (or dogs), a rescue dog – of any breed – is perhaps unwise, unless you are experienced. Territory and status problems can arise, and you must have the experience to understand their body language for any impending trouble. Certainly, a new juvenile or adult dog should be introduced to your other dog(s) away from the home. The dogs should be allowed to meet and mingle on neutral territory and then taken home together. They then need to be watched for a few weeks, to make sure no antagonism develops. This book does not have the scope to dwell on such intricate behavioural issues as pack formation, alpha tendencies and male/female dominance. Safe to say, introducing a new adult to an existing pack is not for the faint hearted. In any case, if you do apply for a rescue dog, then you will probably have been thoroughly vetted beforehand by an expert in the breed, who will have visited your home and would have to be completely satisfied that you and other dog(s) in the house are able to adapt to a new family member.

Introducing a new puppy to other dogs is not usually a problem, although adult dogs will want to examine the newcomer, so don't be surprised if the pup is unceremoniously dumped on his back, so that the adults can give him a good sniffing around his private parts. The puppy will usually submit, and, before long, he will find his limits with the older dog(s) and quickly integrate. A young puppy is full of energy and should not be allowed boisterous, unsupervised play with older dogs, as injuries will undoubtedly follow.

Try not to interfere when the two dogs are getting to know each other – in most cases they will end up the best of friends.

The Rottweiler is generally very tolerant with other dogs, and with tactful handling will accept a newcomer to his family.

HOUSE RULES

You must quickly establish your house rules. Always be gentle but firm with a dog. He must learn where he can and cannot go, and, until you are confident he knows the rules, you will have to watch him every moment. Chairs and settees are yours, not the dog's. Have toys and titbits handy. Chewing is natural for a dog, particularly a teething puppy, so you have to be constantly aware of where the dog is and what he is doing. Don't forget: a quiet puppy is often like a quiet child – up to something! When the dog does something wrong, you must firmly say "No" and mean it, although a dog actually understands tone and sound – not words. If you want take something out of your puppy's mouth, try distracting him with something else that he can chew on or play with, praising him when he does.

A Rottweiler puppy is quick to learn and will soon understand a toileting routine.

NEIGHBOURS

Try to introduce your dog to your neighbours as soon as possible. As the dog establishes himself in your home, he will naturally learn to guard and you want him to realise that the man next door is a friend and not a threat. Unless your neighbours are genuinely afraid of dogs, you should invite them round as soon as the dog has settled. Perhaps they will agree to come at feeding time and actually feed the dog themselves. You never know when you may need their help and you certainly want them to feel safe going into your house in your absence. Some non-dog people are nervous when they hear the word 'Rottweiler' and you will have to get used to this. Unless your neighbours are genuinely afraid of dogs, you should invite them round as soon as the dog has settled. You should be able to show them how friendly the breed really is and this will help alleviate any possible worries. However, if anyone is genuinely afraid of dogs, think hard before they are allowed to meet your dog, particularly if he is an adult. Dogs sense fear and this could trigger a bad reaction.

TOILET TRAINING

Toilet training must start immediately. A puppy is born accepting that bodily functions are allowed whenever and wherever the urge takes him. You have to persuade him otherwise.

At first, a puppy should be taken to the garden regularly, at least every hour or so during the day. Stay with the puppy until he relieves himself. Immediately praise him when he does. Choose a word that you want the dog to associate with toileting. It doesn't matter what the word is, but make sure the whole family knows and uses the same word, so that the dog will come to recognise it.

Try to notice the tell-tale signs and body movements and if you see your dog sniffing or circling indoors, immediately take him to the garden and encourage him with your 'toilet word'. Your puppy will often start to sniff in a particular area, and probably circle. Take him outside when he wakes, after eating or drinking, after a nap, after play, and first thing in the morning/last thing at night. Always use the same spot when you take him out to the garden. Use your 'toilet word' as encouragement and praise him immediately he goes. Puppies love praise, so, hopefully, you should have a clean puppy within a week or two.

It can be disheartening, standing out in the garden in the dark and rain, repeating some phrase such as "Be clean" or "Toilet", while the puppy happily romps around, tearing up your garden plants. But it will be worth it in the end.

Night-time toilet training can be easy and some dogs pick it up very quickly, while others take ages to learn. You have to be patient, as outbursts of temper and punishment will work against you. With a puppy, you are certain to have some mess to clean up in the mornings, for at least a week. Hopefully, the floor of the room your dog is sleeping in is tiled for easy cleaning. Some owners maintain that putting down newspaper trains the dog to use paper as a toilet area. Others argue that this doesn't work, but it does mean the mess is easier to clean up in the morning. If there is a mess, the dog will have no idea why you are angry. Let him out immediately, go with him and be ready to encourage and praise him when he performs in the right place. Then return to the house and clean up the mess quietly and with no fuss.

The rescue dog may already be house-trained. If not, begin the process as you would for a puppy – adopt a regular regime and stick to it. All dogs must be allowed out into the garden as soon as the household is up and about. This is the time when you have a very good chance of success, as the dog will almost certainly urinate immediately. Go with him and be ready to praise. Take your adult dog for a walk as soon as possible. The start of the walk should be brisk if you are in a built-up area, so he doesn't have time to think about squatting. He will soon find out where other dogs have been and, eventually, he should find an area that suits him, and relieve himself. Give the usual praise and lots of encouragement. Don't forget your poop-scoop bag to clean up after your dog. This is a legal requirement.

DAILY ROUTINE

Much like children, a dog tends to thrive most when his life is structured by routine, as this helps him to feel safe and secure and more receptive to new experiences and training.

An older dog will find it easier to settle if you stick to a basic routine.

PUPPY MEALTIMES

Feeding time is a very important part of a dog's day, as you will see when he gets used to the sound of the food bowl. A puppy needs several smaller feeds and you should be guided by the regime of the breeder. You may eventually decide to change the type of food, but if so, then do this gradually and certainly not for a few weeks at least. As a general rule, your young puppy will have three or four meals a day, decreasing to two by the time he is about six months old. A juvenile or adult dog should be fed twice a day. Most dogs are gluttons and will bolt their food if fed once a day only. This can cause problems and should be avoided.

A good time to give the morning feed for puppies is about half an hour after he has been out and running in the garden. For adults, wait until after the morning walk. Never feed before a walk, as this can result in a life-threatening condition called bloat (where the dog's stomach fills with gas and twists). At best, exercise immediately after eating can simply be unpleasant for your dog. The last evening meal should be around 8pm for the young puppy and after the evening walk for the adult. The puppy's other meals should be evenly spread during the day, until he is on two meals a day. The breeder should tell you how much to give at each meal and you can gradually increase this as the puppy grows and you reduce the number of meals.

To begin with, your puppy will need four meals a day.

HANDLING

Accustom a young puppy to all over handling – and give him a reward when he co-operates.

Lift up each paw in turn.

Examine his teeth and gums.

Check your puppy's ears.

EXERCISE

A Rottweiler puppy will get all the exercise he needs from running around in the garden. Neither children nor adult dogs should be allowed to play unsupervised with a puppy in the garden, as injuries may occur. Exhausted puppies will sleep when they want to and wake up for more exploring and running around. The rule is no enforced exercise of any sort.

Very short walks can be taken at about five or six months of age, but these should be on a lead. Gradually build this up to longer distances but it's best not to go too far at first. Do not allow running up and down stairs or jumping in and out of the car. An adult Rottweiler will go any distance you want him to, but any special training (e.g. for working trials or agility) that involves hurdles and scale jumping, should not be attempted until about 20 months.

HANDLING AND TRAINING

Once your new puppy or dog has settled in to the home, you should begin to condition him to being handled all over. There will be times when you have to be hands on, such as removing a thorn from the dog's foot, having him examined by a vet, grooming him, or cutting or filing his nails. There is no point in trying to do this to a grown Rottweiler who is not used to it – you will lose the battle.

The best time to start is perhaps during a quiet spell in the afternoon, or in the evening when you are watching TV. Sit on the floor for a while and encourage the dog to lie between your outstretched legs. He will love it. Then encourage him to lie on his back. Gently rub his chest and belly and you will have him in raptures. Once he is happy with this, start to move your hands gently over his body. Feel

Teach your adult Rottweiler to jump in and out of the car – and to settle quietly in his crate.

each paw and gently press. You should examine every toe individually and be able to scrape the nails. Handle the mouth area until your dog will allow you to examine his teeth. Fondle his ears, then gently wipe inside with a piece of cotton wool. All of these actions should be accompanied by the usual bribery of a small biscuit. This should be an ongoing training process and become part of the daily routine. Your dog should be completely confident that handling is friendly and pain-free.

Don't expect instant success and never make handling a trial of strength; a full-grown

Rottweiler will beat you any day. This procedure will take time to show results, but it should work if you are firm but gentle. Like everything else in a dog's life, you must make it fun and a rewarding experience. Once you have the dog's confidence, you can also start the grooming experience. A stiff grooming brush is needed and when the dog is shedding his coat, you will get enough hair to make a jumper.

TRAVELLING

Apart from taking your dog for walks, there may well be times when you want to go further, in the car. This can be the really

expensive bit. You would not think of leaving a child unrestrained in the rear seat of the car and the same applies to your dog. Apart from the safety of the dog, you have to think of the worst-case scenario if you collide with something or you have to make an emergency stop. Consider the effect of 45 kilos of dog hitting you or your loved ones in the back of the neck, and you will fully understand the need for a cage. There are grilles you can buy that separate the rear section of a hatchback or estate from the passenger area. Otherwise there are wire-mesh, or purpose-made, tough steel cages that fit in the rear of your estate. Your dog will be safe in either option. Do not leave your dog rattling around in the back of the car – it is dangerous for him and you.

If you are thinking "I have a saloon, not a hatchback or estate, what do I do?" The answer is simple – you need to change your car! So, a dog that cost several hundreds of pounds will now cost you several thousands – welcome to the world of dogs.

Once you have the safety issue resolved, you can start to take the dog out in the car. Make it a happy situation. As soon as the dog gets in, give him lots of praise and the standard titbit. Some dogs love car travel – some don't. Like other training, start off a little at a time. Take the dog perhaps a mile to the shops and then to a supermarket car park, so you can walk around for a bit and combine car training with socialisation (see Chapter 6). Gradually lengthen the journeys you make and always have a window open, so fresh air can circulate. If your dog starts to bark, or drools, don't pacify him or you will reinforce his fears/behaviour and he will carry on doing it. With luck, your dog will become a happy passenger in a relatively short period of time.

If you take your dog out in the car and have to leave him in it for short periods while you perform some errands, be very careful. Leave adequate ventilation as, even on a mild day, the temperature inside a car can quickly rise to dangerous levels.

It is in the first few weeks that you establish a bond with your Rottweiler that will last a lifetime.

THE BEST OF CARE

The best of care means many things – good feeding, correct housing (preferably in the home) good socialisation, and, above all, lots of love and attention. A Rottweiler gives a great deal of affection to his family and wants to be part of everything that is going on.

FEEDING METHODS

Giving the best food to your dog is of utmost importance. A reputable breeder would have given the puppies good, wholesome food. When the puppy is ready to go to his new home, the breeder should supply a diet sheet and information about nutrition. The breeder would normally supply enough food to last your puppy about a week. If your puppy is healthy and bright-eyed, it would be best to continue on this diet for a while longer. If you do wish to change the diet to something else, then please make sure you do this very gradually, to save an upset stomach.

There are different feeding regimes and dozens of different brands of dog food manufactured today – some very cheap and some exorbitantly expensive. Sometimes a little experimentation is needed to find which best suits your particular dog and you must do your own research before you decide on which regime to follow. Please note that, whichever way you decide to feed your Rottweiler, you should stick to one method and not combine them, as this could lead to complications. If you wish to change to a different diet, the changeover must be gradual.

COMPLETE (DRIED)

This method of feeding is very popular and contains all the vitamins and nutrients necessary for the dog's wellbeing. However, there are some added E numbers in many of them and several have far too high a protein and fat level than is required. A good guide is between 18 per cent for adults, and 25 per cent protein for puppies. Read the label and see what the product contains. These foods do not require any added supplements. Do not be tempted by the cheaper range – you get what you pay for.

There are a number of holistic products that contain only natural additives, with no E numbers. These are again complete foods and do not require any added supplements. On the whole they are quite expensive, but they are excellent and worth considering if you wish to feed in a natural way without adding raw meat. However, most allow a small

Complete diets are formulated to meet a dog's needs at different stages of his life.

Canned food is convenient to use – but check the nutritional balance.

Most dogs will relish a natural, home-made diet.

THE BARF DIET

This diet is based on the principle of feeding as near to a natural diet as possible. Bones and Raw Food or Biologically Appropriate Raw Food (BARF) includes raw meats and vegetables, but no grain-based carbohydrates. It is said by the originator of the diet (Dr Ian Billinghurst of Australia) that dogs cannot digest carbohydrate, which can cause many health problems, i.e. inflammatory diseases such as pancreatitis. Many people are feeding this diet with apparently good results, but do try to read everything on the subject and talk to people who feed in this way before you give it a try. It requires considerable dedication on the part of the owner to get it right.

Feeding raw vegetables is an extremely important part of a raw diet. Vegetables must never be cooked, as this will destroy the vitamin content. Grating the vegetables is not sufficient either. They must be crushed.

When herbivores (vegetable eaters) eat their food they chew and crush the food many times over (called 'chewing the cud'), which reduces the vegetation to pulp. Your dog cannot easily digest cellulose (plant cells are surrounded by cellulose), which means that, if you feed lumps of raw vegetable, the vast majority (about 99 per cent) of the nutrients contained in that vegetable matter are not passed on to your dog as they pass straight through the digestive system, completely unchanged. Each and every cell of the vegetable has to be released from the cellulose wall that surrounds it, and this means that every cell has to be crushed and split open in order for it to be of any benefit to your dog.

When carnivores (meat eaters) catch their prey and eat it, they also eat the stomach contents of the herbivore (the vegetable eaters), which would have contained the naturally digested vegetable matter. So, in order to reproduce the vegetable pulp as in the wild, a good tip is to put the raw vegetables into a fruit/vegetable juicer, an electric food processor, or an old-fashioned meat mincer, and grind them into a pulp. Do not try to store the vegetable pulp, as it becomes oxidised (goes off very quickly) and loses much of its nutritional value. It must be fed fresh.

If you wish to feed whole, raw chicken or chicken wings, this is fine, but never feed cooked chicken bones to your dog, as they can splinter and pierce the intestines, or cause choking or death.

amount of meat to be added (for variety) without upsetting the balance of the food, should you wish to do this. Again, shop around and read the labels.

Remember: fresh water must be available at all times but particularly if you decide to give dry food.

MEAT AND BISCUIT

There is a very wide range of canned or sachet products available, from cheap to expensive. These contain the vitamins and nutrients required for a reasonably healthy diet, but some are made up of about 80 per cent water. They require the addition of carbohydrate in the form of a mixer biscuit, preferably wholemeal, to give a completely balanced diet. Sometimes people also feed table scraps and tinned fish, and this is perfectly acceptable also.

A Rottweiler puppy has a lot of growing to do, so ideally you want to see gradual weight gain.

AD LIB

Another method of feeding is the so-called 'ad lib' one. This is when dry food is left for the dog to help himself whenever he feels like it. Many investigations have been undertaken, and problems can occur when dogs put on too much weight, as they usually will with this method – have you ever known a healthy dog refuse food? The number of overweight dogs around at the moment is testament to this problem. Observations on the rearing of piglets have shown that many orthopaedic conditions are

caused by allowing the animals to gain weight too quickly. These conditions also occur in dogs, and the best regime for pups is a well-balanced feeding regime, with a gradual weight gain, giving the dog the best chance of reaching adulthood in a healthy and sound way.

NUTRITION

All dogs need about 40 to 43 varied nutrients to remain in good health. These are proteins, carbohydrates, fats, minerals and vitamins.

PROTEINS

These contain the amino acids the body needs, and, during the rapid growth period, proteins are paramount. Chief sources are meat, milk, fish, egg yolk, cereals, cheese and yoghurt. When feeding eggs raw, it is sometimes suggested that only the yolk is given, as the white contains substances that inhibit enzymes and make it difficult for young puppies, sick or old dogs, to digest them. If in doubt, feed the whole egg cooked.

The best source of protein is meat, e.g. beef cheek, and also

A Rottweiler needs a well balanced-diet that is suited to his individual requirements.

chicken and turkey, as they contain approximately the same calorific value as beef. About one-fifth of a dog's daily intake should be protein, and although some excess can be tolerated, it is better to feed less rather than more.

CARBOHYDRATES
About half the dog's daily intake should be made up of carbohydrates. They are an important source of energy and help to regulate the dog's body temperature. A dog not receiving sufficient carbohydrate will use valuable protein to maintain his energy level. Carbohydrates are found in vegetables, but cooked wholegrain cereals are also a very good source. Very little is found in white bread or other refined products. Vitamins are found in the carbohydrates contained in fruit

as well as vegetables, and dogs should be encouraged to eat both. Note: grapes are harmful to dogs.

FATS
Dogs need some fat in their diet, as it is a source of energy. Contrary to common belief, providing some fat will not make a dog overweight. About 8 per cent is acceptable. If a dog has a poor coat, loss of hair, etc., adding a little corn oil or sunflower oil to the food would be beneficial, but the best oil to give is fish oil.

VITAMINS
These are essential, but should not be overdone, and must be fed in a balanced way. A good diet should supply all the vitamins necessary for good health. In certain circumstances

supplementation may be called for, particularly vitamin B, but it is important that the correct diagnosis is made before supplementing a diet. The mistaken belief that 'if a vitamin is good, give a lot', can, in some cases, be extremely detrimental.

- **Vitamin A:** In humans, this vitamin is manufactured in the liver, but a dog's system does not work in this way, so it must be supplied in the diet. Good sources include egg yolk, kidney, meat and cheese. Liver also is an excellent source but this must not be fed in too large a quantity, as it can lead to an upset stomach.
- **Vitamin B:** This vitamin is an important aid to digestion, and if a dog ever has to have antibiotics or sulpha drugs,

Both the quantity of food and the number of meals need to change as a Rottweiler grows.

these can destroy vitamin B. A loss of this vitamin in the body leads to a lowering resistance to infection and disease. Vitamin B12 is in liver, yeast products such as Marmite, brown rice, wheat germ and milk.

- **Vitamin C:** This vitamin plays a small part in the diet. It can be found in fresh fruit. It cannot be stored in the body and is destroyed by cooking. It also helps to form the dentine on teeth. Some time ago it was believed that feeding large amounts of vitamin C could help in the reduction of hip dysplasia, but this has never been conclusively proved.

- **Vitamin D:** This vitamin is very important in the relationship between calcium and phosphorus in the

formation of bone. It is difficult for vitamin D to be extracted from food in large enough quantities, but if a dog is let out in the sun for about two hours a day, this should supply an adequate amount. Vitamin D capsules and tablets are available, but must be fed in the correct quantities. Too much of this vitamin can cause the most horrendous consequences of malabsorption. Perhaps, for the new owner, this is best left alone.

- **Vitamin E:** This vitamin is very important to the function of the body, especially the reproductive system. Foods rich in vitamin E include wheat germ oil, oatmeal, olive oil, whole wheat, eggs and vegetables

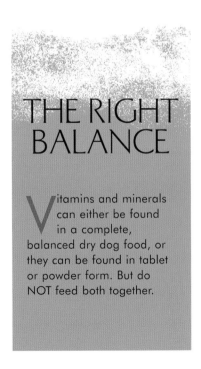

THE RIGHT BALANCE

Vitamins and minerals can either be found in a complete, balanced dry dog food, or they can be found in tablet or powder form. But do NOT feed both together.

such as spinach, carrots, sprouts and parsley.

MINERALS

Calcium and phosphorus: It is important to realise that minerals help to maintain the amount of water necessary for life. Calcium and phosphorus are the most important of the minerals and they are needed in a far greater amount than the others. Both minerals are in the bones and teeth in a chemical combination with vitamin D. The margin of error is very small and this is another area best left alone by the amateur. Indeed, if too much phosphorus and vitamin D are added, disaster can result. The body will draw calcium from the bones and the result is softening of the bones. A puppy is born with cartilage, with only a very small trace of calcium. If the diet is well balanced with the correct ratio of calcium/phosphorus/vitamin D, all will be well. However, if the balance is wrong, all sorts of problems could occur.

Other minerals: The other minerals required in small amounts are manganese, magnesium and iron, which help the oxygen to be transported in the blood. These will occur naturally in a normal diet.

FEEDING REGIME

From around three to four weeks of age, while in the breeder's care, your puppy will have been weaned from mother's milk to solids. Some breeders feed scraped raw beefsteak or finely minced tripe, while others start with a 'complete' weaning porridge and either goat's or dried milk (but definitely not cow's milk). This enables the pups to get used to solid food, as they would in nature.

Both systems are good, but many breeders do not feed milk at all after weaning as, in the natural state, the dam would not want her pups to feed from her and would chastise them if they tried. Many of the specially adapted milk powders are excellent for dogs, and goat's milk is extremely good, being

The Rottweiler is a muscular, powerfully built dog, but he should not carry excess weight.

very mild and gentle to the stomach. Cow's milk goes 'straight through' the system with unpleasant results, so this should be avoided. Cereals in the form of porridge, Weetabix and the like can be fed, but definitely no sugar should be given to the puppy's food, although honey is excellent. Weaning should be very gradual, and eventually, pups at eight weeks should be on four or five meals daily, never less.

Puppies should go on to three meals daily at about 12 weeks, until about seven months, and on to two meals a day from then on. Some adult dogs are fed once a day only, but it is generally accepted that one meal split into two feeds a day is the best option. Feeding a large heavy meal to a large breed such as the Rottweiler can sometimes result in a condition known as bloat (where the stomach becomes filled with gas and twists), which can be fatal. It is also suggested by some that meat and biscuit are not fed together, i.e. breakfast of wholemeal biscuit, perhaps with plain cottage cheese or yoghurt, and an evening meal of raw or other meat. This regime would, of course, need additional supplements.

A rough guide to how much a growing puppy needs is 1 ounce (28 grams) per pound (450g) of bodyweight. This applies to a younger puppy that is growing very quickly. A Rottweiler puppy bitch after eight weeks gains about 2lb (900g) weekly, whereas

WEIGHT TEST

A good way to tell if your puppy is the right weight is to run your hands down the sides. If you can just feel the individual ribs, he is about the right weight – but at six months if he hasn't got a 'waist', he is probably too fat. Bear in mind that Rottweiler puppies can grow at an alarming rate and at four months or so, a Rottweiler will be about half his adult weight. If you have any doubts, ask an experienced breeder or owner.

It is a good idea to weigh your Rottweiler at regular intervals.

a male can increase as much as 3-4lb (1,350-1,800g) a week. The average weight of a bitch puppy at eight weeks is in the region of 10-12lb (4,500-5,400g) and a male 13-15lb (7,200-9,000g). Adult food requirement is about one-third of an ounce per pound (9g per 450g) of bodyweight, but this is for general guidance only and will vary between individual dogs.

Many breeders have the feeding bowl raised (placed on to a metal stand, which raises it off the ground) to suit the individual animal. For a young puppy, this would be at about 20cm (8 inches) . This method can also be used for older dogs to aid digestion and reduce the incidence of bloat.

GROOMING
Conditioning really starts with correct feeding, but a Rottweiler's coat is very easy to maintain through grooming. His coat sheds twice a year and can become unsightly at times, with a greyish, waxy bloom. Regular

combing and brushing will help to improve the problem and remove the dead hairs. For the rest of the year, however, the best method is a walk in the rain and a good rub down afterwards with a towel. This is usually quite sufficient for the Rottweiler's coat to remain shiny and healthy. Bear in mind that too much bathing in the many shampoos that are available in the pet shop can strip the natural oils from the coat with dry, scurfy results.

Grooming is an ideal time to check for fleas, lice and ticks, which are easy to eradicate. Also, check for bumps and lumps on the dog's skin; many of these are harmless, such as some forms of cysts, but others may not be. A veterinary surgeon should always be consulted if any are found. Your vet will also be able to advise you about routine parasite control (fleas and worms).

TEETH

A Rottweiler's first teeth start to come through at about the same time as the eyes open and the hearing develops, at about two weeks old. The second teeth erupt at about four months, but some of the teeth can come through as late as nine months. It is never too early to start cleaning them, which gets the pup used to the mouth being touched. Make sure you do so gently and don't grip or force open the mouth. Try touching a tooth, then give lots of praise; then, next day, touch two teeth, and so on until the pup is quite happy for you to handle his mouth. At the same time, gently but firmly dissuade him from mouthing or biting – this will be invaluable when he is older. Then try the toothbrush very gently on one tooth, and so on. This is far better than gripping the mouth open, forcing the issue, as a Rottweiler will soon resent this. If you intend to show your dog, this procedure must be carried out in a calm and sensitive way.

NAILS

The nails of an adult Rottweiler are extremely tough and hard and can grow quite long if the dog is not exercised on a hard surface. They should be kept as short as possible. This is especially relevant if you have a grassy garden, or if your walks are taken on a grassy footpath or over the countryside. Nails can be snipped on a young puppy very easily, using an ordinary pair of human nail clippers.

As the puppy grows and the nails become harder, you will need the strongest set of animal nail clippers that you can find. Some nails seem to grow at an alarming rate and need shortening frequently, which quite often happens if the foot is flat or splayed. If the foot is tight and catlike, the nails don't seem to grow very much at all.

A problem can occur with the front dewclaws. If left too long, they can curl round and grow back in to the leg, which can be very painful.

Many Rottweilers do not like their feet being held or having their nails trimmed, so problems can arise. It is best to overcome this by accustoming your Rottweiler puppy to having his feet handled from the very beginning.

When clipping your dog's nails, try not to cut into the 'quick', as this will bleed a lot and can put a dog off having his nails done another time. Do take off the pointy tip to leave a neat, trimmed foot, but, if in doubt, ask your breeder or vet to show you how.

Another method is to use a large metal file, which is easier. If all else fails, your veterinary surgeon will do the job for you at a price. There is a battery-powered tool on the market, which is rather like a small grinder. It is apparently effective if you can train your dog to sit still long enough, but this machine is rather expensive.

ROUTINE CARE

The Rottweiler has a low-maintenance coat, and needs no more than regular brushing to remove the dead hairs.

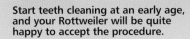

Start teeth cleaning at an early age, and your Rottweiler will be quite happy to accept the procedure.

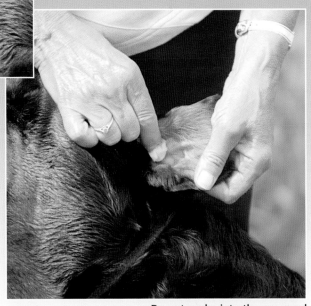

Do not probe into the ear canal when you are cleaning ears.

Regular brushing and checking of a dog's teeth can often prevent expensive visits to the vet. There are many types of toothpaste for dogs for brushing and others where you do not need a brush at all. Large raw bones or the many manufactured bones are all good for the teeth, although they are no substitute for regular brushing.

EARS

Ears should be kept as clean as possible in order that ear mites or canker do not build up and cause the ears to smell. One sure sign of a problem is when the dog continually shakes his head and hangs his ear down on one side of the head.

You should not try to sort out the condition by yourself, and your vet should be consulted. It is acceptable to gently wipe around the inner surface of the ear with witch hazel on a piece of cotton wool (never use cotton ear buds) and never poke down inside. There are various wipes containing gentle cleansing agents and these are very good to use two or three times a week.

EYES

These should be clear and bright without any stickiness or discharge. There are one or two eye conditions that affect the Rottweiler that are not seen as much these days, but it is as well to know about them. The first is a condition called entropion where the eyelids roll inwards. As a result, the eyelashes rub against the eye, causing pain and ulceration. The other condition is ectropion, where the eyelids roll outwards and allow dust and debris to accumulate in the bottom of the eyelid, causing constant redness and weeping. Both defects are inherited and can be corrected by a specialist veterinary surgeon. Dogs carrying these faults should never be bred from.

EXERCISE AND PLAY

A well-walked dog is a happy dog and has less energy left to devote to mischief. Walking should be done at least twice a day an hour or more *before* or after meals. Before long your garden should become cleaner and you will have a well-trained dog. Use your daily walks to practise some training, such as the recall (see Chapter 6). It is unwise to let a rescue dog off the lead at first. Wait until you are sure of his temperament and you are confident he will come back when you call. Give him as much walking as you have the time and energy for.

Swimming is another very popular exercise, and is also used for therapy after injuries. Some Rottweilers absolutely love swimming, but others will not even get their feet wet, let alone put their whole body into the water. Their first encounter with

A puppy will get all the exercise he needs from playing in the garden.

EXERCISE AND PLAY

Combining physical exertion with mental stimulation
is the perfect way to exercise a Rottweiler.

If you have more than one dog, they will help to exercise each other.

water is always very interesting – try walking a puppy through a puddle, first.

HAVING FUN

All puppies love to play – or they should. There are lots of very good toys for dogs on the market, but make sure they are safe. Tragic accidents have happened when dogs have been allowed to play with balls that have become lodged in the throat and caused the dog to choke to death. Always make sure any toy is quite a lot larger than the dog's mouth.

Another very popular play toy is a rope, which a puppy loves to hang on to with you on the other end. However, do not pull too vigorously while your puppy is teething, in case you damage his teeth. Make sure that the dog stops tugging when you say so, otherwise this is one way a dog learns that very often he can get the better of you. The human must always win any game with toys, not the dog.

Try putting your Rottweiler outside a room and then hide toys or food for him to find. Make sure you reward him when he does, and he will always be eager to please and play the game again. When out for walks, drop something familiar to the dog (an old glove, for example) and get the dog to follow the trail and find the object. This can be great fun for you and the dog. Do not forget the treat for finding.

Training for obedience and working trials is very rewarding, but hard work. The standards are very high, and to do well requires time and dedication. Agility competition is also popular. As previously stated, jumping should not be undertaken until about 20 months of age. The Kennel Club will give information on all these activities and there is more information in Chapter 6.

A Rottweiler loves to play. He adapts very easily to any lifestyle, and he is happy to be with you

If you keep your Rottweiler lean and fit, he will remain active for much longer.

whatever you are doing. The Rottweiler is an intelligent dog and the more activity you can give him, the better. A bored Rottweiler is not a happy dog and will get up to all sorts of mischief if allowed. This is when a lot of the behaviour problems occur, so the mind must be kept active or things can happen, through no fault of the dog.

This is a wonderful breed and it deserves the best owners. A well-balanced Rottweiler is a joy to own, giving love and devotion in spades – so don't let him down!

CARING FOR THE OLDER DOG

There are many diets on the market for the 'senior' dog. There is a vast price range and most are very expensive – so if in doubt, always consult your vet.

Although it is important that your dog is fed well, he should not be allowed to get overweight, and this should be the case at all ages. If your dog is healthy, he will take as much food as you will offer him, but this is not always a good thing and care must be taken to ensure he does not become fat and lethargic. The Rottweiler is a very greedy dog and experience shows that some dogs seem to eat just as much when they are older as when they were young. Remember that having a dog overweight will place a burden on his joints and heart.

Dogs can remain active up to 10 or even 11 years of age and it can be difficult to guess their age. On the whole, requirements for food should be tailored to suit individual dogs. Generally, dogs require less as they age.

One of the many problems that can affect older dogs is arthritis,

The needs of your Rottweiler will change as he becomes older.

which can slow them down. The easy option is to not to exercise them, but as is the case for humans, the advice is to keep the dog active and not let the joints seize up. There are many things that can be given to alleviate this problem and your vet should always be consulted.

Older dogs probably will sleep a lot more, but experience shows Rottweilers will sleep anywhere, any time, until you want to take them out or do other interesting things. Your older dog will still want to be included and should not be left out of family events just because he is a bit slower.

This is the same dog you loved as a puppy, so your feelings towards him shouldn't change.

Unfortunately, something that very often happens to the older dog is urinary incontinence. A dog hates it when this happens and it can prove very distressing to care for. Your veterinary surgeon should be consulted, as there are drugs that can help. One thing that can be done is to restrict water intake late at night and to increase the frequency with which you take your Rottweiler outside to relieve himself.

As a dog gets older his eyesight

can sometimes fail. Cataracts or other defects can be a problem, and this can mean the dog becomes distressed if furniture and other objects are changed around. Fortunately, this is usually compensated for by the dog's sense of smell, which is far better than ours. Before approaching a dog, let him know you are around by speaking to him, which will help him to adjust to the situation. Obviously he will find it difficult to move around a garden if implements are left for him to tread on, so tidy up and make sure everything is safe for the dog. Talk to other owners who have had this problem to deal with, as people are always willing to give advice.

Sometimes the dog may lose his sense of hearing, and, should this happen, he will need a lot of reassurance. Any commands given would have to be seen by him and a lot of patience is required especially when out walking. Discuss this with your veterinary surgeon, as advice can be given on how to cope with this condition.

These are just some of the conditions you may have to deal with in the older dog, but often sight and hearing remains intact, and some never suffer from incontinence. It is, however, always best to be prepared. Patience and understanding is needed at all times. Your dog will have given you his undying devotion throughout his life, and it is now your turn to repay this.

SAYING GOODBYE

When the time comes to have to say goodbye to your best friend, you must think of the dog's quality of life and not your own emotions. Making the decision to have your dog euthanased is the hardest part. Don't let your old friend struggle on day after day, suffering the indignity of you having to hold him up whilst he toilets in the garden. This is no life for your best friend. One day your dog may look at you and deep within his eyes you will know that he really is tired of life. This is the time to let him go.

If appropriate, arrangements can be made with your vet to visit your home when you feel the time is right. Keep your dog calm, lay him out on a blanket, cradle his head in your lap and tell him how much he has enriched your life, and how glad you have been to be a part of it. Try not to cry as this will add to the stress level for the dog. The dog itself will have no idea of what he is about to face – just a simple injection and he will fade away into a deep sleep.

In time you will be able to look back on all the happy times you spent with your Rottweiler.

TRAINING AND SOCIALISATION

Chapter 6

When you decided to bring a Rottweiler into your life, you probably had dreams of how it was going to be: long walks together, cosy evenings with a Rottweiler lying devotedly at your feet, and whenever you returned home, there would always be a special welcome waiting for you.

There is no doubt that you can achieve all this – and much more – with a Rottweiler, but like anything that is worth having, you must be prepared to put in the work. A Rottweiler, regardless of whether it is a puppy or an adult, does not come ready trained, understanding exactly what you want and fitting perfectly into your lifestyle. A Rottweiler has to learn his place in your family and he must discover what is acceptable behaviour.

We have a great starting point in that the Rottweiler has an outstanding temperament. He thrives on human companionship and loves to learn. This is a dog who is calm, intelligent and highly motivated. However, it is also important to bear in mind that the Rottweiler is a powerful dog, bred to drive cattle and to guard. He is a tough dog, both physically and mentally, and so an extensive programme of training and socialisation is essential in order to bring out the best in this magnificent breed.

THE FAMILY PACK
Dogs have been domesticated for some 14,000 years, but, luckily for us, they have inherited and retained behaviour from their distant ancestor – the wolf. A Rottweiler may never have lived in the wild, but he is born with the survival skills and the mentality of a meat-eating

predator who hunts in a pack. A wolf living in a pack owes its existence to mutual co-operation and an acceptance of a hierarchy, as this ensures both food and protection. A domesticated dog living in a family pack has exactly the same outlook. He wants food, companionship, and leadership – and it is your job to provide for these needs.

YOUR ROLE
Theories about dog behaviour and methods of training go in and out of fashion, but in reality, nothing has changed from the day when wolves ventured in from the wild to join the family circle. The wolf (and equally the dog) accepts a co-operative place in the family pack in return for food and protection. In a dog's eyes, you are his leader, and he relies on you to make all the important decisions. This does not mean that you have to act like a dictator

or a bully. You are accepted as a leader, without argument, as long as you have the right credentials.

The first part of the job is easy. You are the provider, and you are therefore respected because you supply food. The second part of the leader's job description is straightforward, but for some reason we find it hard to achieve. In order for a dog to accept his place in the family pack he must respect his leader as the decision-maker. A happy, confident and positively trained dog does not question authority; he is perfectly happy to see someone else shoulder the responsibility. Problems will only arise if you cut a poor figure as leader and the dog feels he should make the decisions.

Can you be a firm, fair and consistent leader?

HOW TO BE A GOOD LEADER

There are a number of guidelines to follow to establish yourself in the role of leader in a way that your Rottweiler understands and respects. If you have a puppy, you may think you don't have to take this on board for a few months, but that would be a big mistake. Start as you mean to go on, and your pup will be quick to find his place in his new family.

- **Keep it simple:** Decide on the rules you want your Rottweiler to understand and always make it 100 per cent clear what is acceptable, and what is unacceptable, behaviour.
- **Be consistent:** If you are not consistent about enforcing rules, how can you expect your Rottweiler to take you seriously? There is nothing worse than allowing your Rottweiler to jump up at you one moment and then scolding him the next time he does it because you were wearing your best clothes. As far as the Rottweiler is concerned, he may as well try it on because he can't predict your reaction.
- **Get your timing right:** If you are rewarding your Rottweiler, and equally if you are interrupting undesirable behaviour, you must respond within one to two seconds or the dog will not link his behaviour with your reaction (see page 91).
- **Read your dog's body language:** Find out how to read body language and facial expressions so that you understand your Rottweiler's feelings and his intentions.
- **Be aware of your own body language:** When you ask your Rottweiler to do something, try not to bend over him and talk at him. As far as a Rottweiler is concerned, 'eyeballing' is perceived as threatening. It is important to remember that the Rottweiler is a guarding breed, and he may become defensive if

88

he feels threatened. When you are interacting with your Rottweiler maintain a relaxed posture, don't stare at him, and try to stand slightly sideways. You can also help your dog to learn by using your body language to communicate with him. For example, if you want your dog to come to you, open your arms out and look inviting. If you want your dog to stay, use a hand signal (palm flat, facing the dog) so you are effectively 'blocking' his advance. But always blink and smile so you are non-threatening.

- **Tone of voice:** Dogs are very receptive to tone of voice, so you can use your voice to praise him or to correct undesirable behaviour. If you are pleased with your Rottweiler, praise him to the skies in a warm, happy voice. If you want to stop him raiding the bin, say "No" in a calm voice, and then recall him to you with praise.

- **Give one command only:** If you keep repeating a command, or keep changing it, your Rottweiler will think you are babbling and will probably ignore you. If your Rottweiler does not respond the first time you ask, make it simple by using a treat to lure him into position, and then you can reward him for a correct response.

- **Daily reminders:** A young, exuberant Rottweiler is apt to forget his manners from time to time, and an adolescent dog may attempt to challenge your

Be aware of your body language, as a Rottweiler will respond more strongly to this than to verbal communication.

authority (see page 104). Rather than coming down on your Rottweiler like a ton of bricks when he does something wrong, try to prevent bad manners by daily reminders of good manners. For example:

i   Do not let your dog barge ahead of you when you are going through a door.
ii Do not let him leap out of the car the moment you open the door (which could be potentially lethal, as well as being disrespectful).
iii At first, try not to feed

treats by hand since this may encourage a puppy to grab at children's fingers. Food can become a contentious issue among dogs because they are born scavengers. If you watch puppies in a litter, they will instinctively squabble among themselves to get to the food first. Reward your Rottweiler by dropping food on the floor, and then he will return to you to look for more. You are the provider – but he will learn that he cannot mug you to get what he wants.

In order to understand your Rottweiler, you need to see the world from his perspective.

UNDERSTANDING YOUR ROTTWEILER

Body language is an important means of communication between dogs, which they use to make friends, to assert status, and to avoid conflict. It is important to get on your dog's wavelength by understanding his body language and reading his facial expressions.

- A positive body posture, with head held high, indicates a happy, confident dog.

- A crouched body posture with ears back show that a dog is feeling insecure. A dog may do this when he is being told off or if a more assertive dog approaches him.
- A bold dog will stand tall, looking strong and alert, with his ears forward.
- A dog who raises his hackles (lifting the fur along his topline) is trying to look as scary as possible. This may be the prelude to aggressive behaviour, but, in many cases,

the dog is apprehensive and is unsure how to cope with a situation.
- A playful dog will go down on his front legs while standing on his hind legs in a bow position. This friendly invitation says: "I'm no threat, let's play."
- A tense, aggressive dog will meet other dogs with a hard stare. If he is challenged, he may bare his teeth and growl, and the corners of his mouth will be drawn forward. His ears will be forward and he will appear tense in every muscle.
- A nervous dog will often show aggressive behaviour as a means of self-protection. If nervous or apprehensive, a Rottweiler will stand tall with a rigid body, and will stare intently (see A Helping Hand, page 103)

MEETINGS AND GREETINGS

The Rottweiler is a big, powerful dog, and he can be intimidating. Other dogs do not always find a Rottweiler easy to 'read', as he has a dark face, dark eyes, drop ears and, in most cases, no tail. This means that a dog may have to come up close to pick up signals, and inevitably there is a danger of misinterpretation.

A Rottweiler must learn to interact with other dogs, and to show non-threatening behaviour. This is best achieved by taking your Rottweiler to puppy socialisation classes (see below) where he will be exposed to youngsters of a similar age in a controlled environment. He will

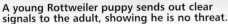

A young Rottweiler puppy sends out clear signals to the adult, showing he is no threat.

Two adults meet, but their intentions are friendly.

also learn how to play with other dogs (see Playing with Other Dogs, page 108).

People also have difficulty 'reading' the Rottweiler. A calm, confident dog may not show typical greeting behaviour, such as coming forward, wagging his rear, and looking appeasing. The Rottweiler is a more self-contained dog, and, again, people can find his cool attitude somewhat daunting. The natural reaction is to bend over the dog, engage eye contact, and then try to talk to him. But this can exacerbate the situation.

The Rottweiler is a guarding breed and is very aware of behaviour that may be potentially threatening. He interprets eye contact as a direct threat, and even if you are bending over him, telling him he is a "good boy", he will ignore the verbal

communication and focus on the perceived threat that you pose. Just as the Rottweiler needs to learn how to greet other dogs, he must learn to greet and accept strangers or visitors in a relaxed, happy fashion.

One way of achieving this goal is to recruit some helpers who can come to your house. Ask your helpers to ring the doorbell, walk past your dog and throw some treats on his bed, without making eye contact or any form of physical contact. This scenario should be repeated as many as 10 times in a row. Gradually the friends can stop and look silently at the dog before throwing the treats. By the end of the training session, the Rottweiler will have made a good association with visitors coming to the house, and will not feel threatened in any way.

GIVING REWARDS

Why should your Rottweiler do as you ask? If you follow the guidelines given above, your Rottweiler should respect your authority, but what about the time when he is playing with a new doggy friend or has found a really enticing scent? The answer is that you must always be the most interesting, the most attractive, and the most irresistible person in your Rottweiler's eyes. It would be nice to think you could achieve this by personality alone, but most of us need a little extra help. You need to find out what is the biggest reward for your dog – in a Rottweiler's case, it will nearly always be food – and to give him a treat when he does as you ask. For some dogs, the reward might be a play with a favourite toy, but, whatever it is,

The Rottweiler is highly intelligent and relishes the opportunity to learn something new.

it must be something that your dog really wants.

When you are teaching a dog a new exercise, you should reward him frequently. When he knows the exercise or command, reward him randomly so that he keeps on responding to you in a positive manner. If your dog does something extra special, like leaving his canine chum mid-play in the park, make sure he really knows how pleased you are by giving him a handful of treats or throwing his ball a few extra times. If he gets a bonanza reward, he is more likely to come back on future occasions, because you have proved to be even more rewarding than his previous activity.

TOP TREATS
Some trainers grade treats depending on what they are asking the dog to do. A dog may get a low-grade treat, such as a piece of dry food, to reward good behaviour on a random basis, such as sitting when you open a door or allowing you to examine his teeth. But high-grade treats, which may be cooked liver, sausage or cheese, are reserved for training new exercises or for use in the park when you want a

really good recall. Whatever type of treat you use, remember to subtract it from your Rottweiler's daily ration, or better still, use part of the dog's ration as treats. Fat Rottweilers are lethargic, prone to health problems, and will almost certainly have a shorter life expectancy. Reward your Rottweiler, but always keep a check on his figure!

HOW DO DOGS LEARN?

It is not difficult to get inside your Rottweiler's head and understand how he learns, as it is not dissimilar to the way we learn. Dogs learn by conditioning: they find out that specific behaviours produce specific consequences. This is known as operant conditioning or consequence learning. Consequences have to be immediate or clearly linked to the behaviour, as a dog sees the world in terms of action and result. Dogs will quickly learn if an action has a bad consequence or a good consequence.

Dogs also learn by association. This is known as classical conditioning or association learning. It is the type of learning made famous by Pavlov's experiment with dogs. Pavlov presented dogs with food and measured their salivary response (how much they drooled). Then he rang a bell just before presenting the food. At first, the dogs did not salivate until the food was presented. But after a while they learnt that the sound of the bell meant that food was coming, and so they salivated when they heard the bell. A dog needs to learn the association in order for it to have any meaning. For example, a dog that has never seen a lead before will be completely indifferent to it. A dog that has learnt that a lead means he is going for a walk will get excited the second he sees the lead; he has learnt to associate a lead with a walk.

BE POSITIVE

The most effective method of training dogs is to use their ability to learn by consequence and to teach that the behaviour you want produces a good consequence. For example, if you ask your Rottweiler to "Sit", and reward him with a treat, he will learn that it is worth his while to sit on command because it will lead to a treat. He is far more likely to repeat the behaviour, and the behaviour will become stronger, because it results in a positive outcome. This method of training is known as positive reinforcement, and it generally leads to a happy, co-operative dog that is willing to work, and a handler who has fun in training their dog.

The opposite approach is punishment-based training. This is far less effective and often results in a poor relationship between dog and owner. In this method of training, you ask your Rottweiler to "Sit", and, if he does not respond, you deliver a sharp yank on the training collar or push his rear to the ground. The dog learns that not responding to your command has a bad consequence, and he may be more likely to ignore you in the future. However, it may well have a bad consequence for you, too. A dog that is treated in this way may associate harsh handling with the handler and become aggressive or fearful. Instead of establishing a pattern of willing co-operation, you are establishing a relationship built on coercion.

THE CLICKER REVOLUTION

Karen Pryor pioneered the technique of clicker training when she was working with dolphins. It is very much a continuation of Pavlov's work and makes full use of association learning.

Karen wanted to mark 'correct' behaviour at the precise moment it happened. She found it was impossible to toss a fish to a dolphin when it was in mid-air, when she wanted to reward it. Her aim was to establish a conditioned response so the dolphin knew that it had performed correctly and a reward would follow.

The solution was the clicker: a small matchbox-shaped training aid, with a metal tongue that makes a click when it is pressed. To begin with, the dolphin had to learn that a click meant that food was coming. The dolphin then learnt that it

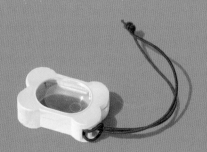

must 'earn' a click in order to get a reward. Clicker training has been used with many different animals, most particularly with dogs, and it has proved hugely successful. It is a great aid for pet owners and is also widely used by professional trainers who teach highly specialised skills.

GETTING STARTED

As you train your Rottweiler, you will develop your own techniques as you get to know what motivates him. You may decide to get involved with clicker training or you may prefer to go for a simple command-and-reward formula. It does not matter what form of training you use, as long as it is based on positive, reward-based methods.

There are a few important guidelines to bear in mind when you are training your Rottweiler:

- Find a training area that is free from distractions, particularly when you are just starting out.
- Keep training sessions short – no more than five minutes – especially with young puppies that have very short attention spans.

- Do not train if you are in a bad mood or if you are on a tight schedule – the training session will be doomed to failure.
- If you are using a toy as a reward, make sure it is only available when you are training. In this way it has an added value for your Rottweiler.
- If you are using food treats, make sure they are bite-size and easy to swallow; you don't want to hang about while your Rottweiler chews on his treat.
- All food treats must be deducted from your Rottweiler's daily food ration or, better still, use the dog's food as treats instead of feeding from the bowl.
- When you are training, move around and practise in lots of different locations so that your dog does not think that an exercise can only be performed in one place.
- If your Rottweiler is finding an exercise difficult, try not to get frustrated. Go back a step and praise him for his effort. You will probably find he is more successful when you try again at the next training session.
- Always end training sessions on a happy, positive note. Ask your Rottweiler to do something you know he can do – it could be a trick he enjoys performing – and then reward him with a few treats or an extra-long play session.

In the exercises that follow, clicker training is introduced and followed, but all the exercises will work without the use of a clicker.

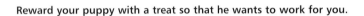
Reward your puppy with a treat so that he wants to work for you.

INTRODUCING A CLICKER

Introducing a clicker is dead easy, and your ever-hungry Rottweiler will learn about the clicker in record time! It can be combined with attention training, which is a very useful tool and can be used on many different occasions.

- Prepare some treats and go to an area that is free from distractions. When your Rottweiler stops sniffing around and looks at you, click and reward by throwing him a treat. This means he will not crowd you, but will go looking for the treat. Repeat a couple of times. If your Rottweiler is very easily distracted, you may need to start this exercise with the dog on a lead.

- After a few clicks, your Rottweiler understands that if he hears a click, he will get a treat. He must now learn that he must 'earn' a click. This time, when your Rottweiler looks at you, wait a little longer before clicking, and then reward him. If your Rottweiler is on a lead but responding well, try him off the lead.

- When your Rottweiler is working for a click and giving you his attention, you can introduce a cue or command word, such as "Watch". Repeat a few times, using the cue. You now have a Rottweiler that understands the clicker and will give you his attention when you ask him to "Watch".

TRAINING EXERCISES

THE SIT

This is the easiest exercise to teach, so it is rewarding for both you and your Rottweiler.

- Choose a tasty treat and hold it just above your puppy's nose. As he looks up at the treat, he will naturally go into the Sit. As soon as your Rottweiler is in position, reward him.

- Repeat the exercise, and when your pup understands what you want, introduce the "Sit" command.

- You can practise at mealtimes by holding out the bowl and waiting for your dog to sit. Most Rottweilers learn this one very quickly!

As soon as your Rottweiler understands what you want, you will not need to lure him with a treat.

Lower a treat towards the ground, and your Rottweiler will follow it and go into the Down position.

THE DOWN
Work hard at this exercise because a reliable Down is useful in many different situations, and an instant Down can be a lifesaver.

- You can start with your dog in a Sit, or it is just as effective to teach it when the dog is standing. Hold a treat just below your puppy's nose, and slowly lower it towards the ground. The treat acts as a lure, and your puppy will follow it, first going down on his forequarters, and then bringing his hindquarters down as he tries to get the treat.
- Make sure you close your fist around the treat, and only reward your puppy with the treat when he is in the correct position. If your puppy is reluctant to go Down, you can apply gentle pressure on his shoulders to encourage him to go into the correct position.
- When your puppy is following the treat and going into position, introduce a verbal command.
- Build up this exercise gradually, each time waiting a little longer before giving the reward, so the puppy learns to stay in the Down position.

THE RECALL
It is never too soon to start training the Recall. In fact, if you have a puppy it is best to start almost from the moment the puppy arrives home, as he has a strong instinct to follow you. Make sure you are always happy and excited when your Rottweiler comes to you, even if he has been slower than you would like. Your Rottweiler must believe that the greatest reward is coming to you.

- You can start teaching the Recall from the moment your puppy arrives home. He will naturally follow you, so keep calling his name and rewarding him when he comes to you.
- Practise in the garden, and when your puppy is busy exploring, get his attention by calling his name; as he runs towards you, introduce the verbal command "Come". Make sure you sound happy

SECRET WEAPON

You can build up a strong Recall by using another form of association learning. Buy a whistle and peep on it when you are giving your Rottweiler his food. You can choose the type of signal you want to give: two short peeps or one long whistle, for example. Within a matter of days, your dog will learn that the sound of the whistle means that food is coming.

Now transfer the lesson outside. Arm yourself with some tasty treats and the whistle. Allow your Rottweiler to run free in the garden, and, after a couple of minutes, use the whistle. The dog has already learnt to associate the whistle with food, so he will come towards you. Immediately reward him

with a treat and lots of praise. Repeat the lesson a few times in the garden so you are confident that your dog is responding before trying it in the park. Make sure you always have some treats in your pocket when you go for a walk, and your dog will quickly learn how rewarding it is to come to you.

and exciting, so your puppy wants to come to you. When he responds, give him lots of praise.

- If your puppy is slow to respond, try running away a few paces, or jumping up and down. It doesn't matter how silly you look; the key issue is to get your puppy's attention, and then make yourself irresistible!
- In a dog's mind, coming when called should be regarded as the best fun because he knows he is always going to be rewarded. Never make the mistake of telling your dog off, no matter how slow he is to respond, as you will undo all your previous hard work.
- When you are free-running

your dog, make sure you have his favourite toy or a pocket full of treats so you can reward him at intervals throughout the walk when you call him to you. Do not allow your dog to free run and only call him back at the end of the walk to clip his lead on. An intelligent Rottweiler will soon realise that the Recall means the end of his walk, and then end of fun – so who can blame him for not wanting to come back?

TRAINING LINE

This is the equivalent of a very long lead, which you can buy at a pet store, or you can make your own with a length of rope. The training line is attached to your Rottweiler's collar and

should be around 15 feet (4.5 metres) in length.

The purpose of the training line is to prevent your Rottweiler from disobeying you so that he never has the chance to get into bad habits. For example, when you call your Rottweiler and he ignores you, you can immediately pick up the end of the training line and call him again. By picking up the line you will have attracted his attention, and if you call in an excited, happy voice, your Rottweiler will come to you. The moment he comes to you, give him a tasty treat so he is instantly rewarded for making the 'right' decision.

The training line is very useful when your Rottweiler becomes an adolescent and is testing your

Start by getting your Rottweiler's attention focused on you.

This is beautiful heelwork – most pet owners would not aspire to such a high standard, but the aim is for your dog to walk on a loose lead, paying attention to you when requested.

leadership. When you have reinforced the correct behaviour a number of times, your dog will build up a strong recall and you will not need to use a training line.

WALKING ON A LOOSE LEAD

This is a simple exercise, which baffles many Rottweiler owners. In most cases, owners are too impatient, wanting to get on with the expedition rather that training the dog how to walk on a lead. Take time with this one; the Rottweiler is a very strong dog,

and a Rottweiler that pulls on the lead is no pleasure to own.

- In the early stages of lead training, allow your puppy to pick his route and follow him. He will get used to the feeling of being 'attached' to you, and has no reason to put up any resistance.
- Next, find a toy or a tasty treat and show it to your puppy. Let him follow the treat/toy for a few paces, and then reward him.
- Build up the amount of time your pup will walk with you,

and when he is walking nicely by your side, introduce the verbal command "Heel" or "Close". Give lots of praise when your pup is in the correct position.
- When your pup is walking alongside you, keep focusing his attention on you by using his name, and then reward him when he looks at you. If it is going well, introduce some changes of direction.
- Do not attempt to take your puppy out on the lead until you have mastered the basics at

Build up the Stay exercise in easy stages.

home. You need to be confident that your puppy accepts the lead and will focus his attention on you when requested before you face the challenge of a busy environment.

• As your Rottweiler gets bigger and stronger, he may try to pull on the lead, particularly if you are heading somewhere he wants to go, such as the park. If this happens, stop, call your dog to you, and do not set off again until he is in the correct position. It may take time, but your Rottweiler will eventually realise that it is more productive to walk by your side than to pull ahead.

STAYS
This may not be the most exciting exercise, but it is one of the most useful. There are many occasions when you want your Rottweiler to stay in position, even if it is only for a few seconds. The classic example is when you want your Rottweiler to stay in the back of the car until you have clipped on his lead. Some trainers use the verbal command "Stay" when the dog is to stay in position for an extended period of time, and "Wait" if the dog is to stay in position for a few seconds until you give the next command. Other trainers use a universal "Stay" to cover all situations. It all comes down to personal preference, and as long as you are consistent, your dog will understand the command he is given.

• Put your puppy in a Sit or a Down, and use a hand signal (flat palm, facing the dog) to show he is to stay in position. Step a pace away from the dog. Wait a second, step back and reward him. If you have a lively pup, you may find it easier to train this exercise on the lead.

• Repeat the exercise, gradually increasing the distance you can leave your dog. When you return to your dog's side, praise him quietly, and release him with a command, such as "OK".

• Remember to keep your body language very still when you are training this exercise, and avoid eye contact with your dog. Work on this exercise over a period of time, and you will build up a really reliable Stay.

SOCIALISATION

The key to owning a well-adjusted dog is to work on a comprehensive programme of socialisation. This is important for all dogs, but with a Rottweiler it is vital. In today's society, the Rottweiler is a challenging breed to own, and it is your duty to give your dog every opportunity to learn about and understand the world he lives in.

When you take on a Rottweiler, he is not only becoming a part of your home and family, he is becoming a member of the community. He needs to be able to live in the outside world, coping calmly with every new situation that comes his way. It is your job to introduce him to as many different experiences as possible and to encourage him to behave in an appropriate manner.

In order to socialise your Rottweiler effectively, it is helpful to understand how his brain is developing, and then you will get a perspective on how he sees the world.

CANINE SOCIALISATION
(Birth to 7 weeks)

This is the time when a dog learns how to be a dog. By interacting with his mother and his littermates, a young pup learns about leadership and submission. He learns to read body posture so that he understands the intentions of his mother and his siblings. A puppy that is taken away from his litter too early may always have behavioural problems with other dogs, either being fearful or aggressive.

Many breeders make the mistake of thinking that Rottweiler puppies only need limited socialisation within the home, and do not take pups out and about before they go to their new owners. This is a big mistake, as there is a vital learning period between three and five weeks. A reputable Rottweiler breeder should take on the task of early socialisation, which includes exposure to new people and places, and to the sound of traffic. This is not difficult to achieve: the breeder can take a small puppy out in

Interaction between littermates is an important part of the learning process.

the car, and then sit on a bench and hold the pup while he absorbs the passing scene. It only takes a few minutes every few days. Equally, the breeder can put the puppy in a rucksack, first making sure he is safe and secure, and go for a short walk so the puppy starts getting used to the everyday sights and sounds of the outside world.

SOCIALISATION PERIOD (7 to 12 weeks)

This is the time when a puppy usually goes to his new home, and so it is the time to get cracking and introduce your Rottweiler puppy to as many different experiences as possible. This includes meeting different people (wearing hats, turbans, carrying sticks, holding umbrellas, etc.), other dogs and animals, seeing new sights, and hearing a range of sounds, from the vacuum cleaner to the roar of traffic. At this stage, a puppy learns very quickly and what he learns will stay with him for the rest of his life.

Obviously, you need to be careful with your puppy before he is fully vaccinated, but this does not mean keeping him shut away from the world.

FEAR-IMPRINT PERIOD (8 to 11 weeks)

This occurs during the socialisation period, and it can be the cause of problems if it is not handled carefully. If a pup is exposed to a frightening or painful experience, it will lead to lasting impressions. Obviously,

There will be signs of a puppy becoming more independent from 12 weeks onwards.

you will attempt to avoid frightening situations, such as your pup being bullied by a mean-spirited older dog, or a firework going off, but you cannot always protect your puppy from the unexpected. If your pup has a nasty experience, the best plan is to make light of it and distract him by offering him a treat or a game. The pup will take the lead from you and will be reassured that there is nothing to worry about. If you mollycoddle him and sympathise with him, he is far more likely to retain the memory of his fear.

SENIORITY PERIOD (12 to 16 weeks)

During this period, your Rottweiler puppy starts to cut the apron strings and becomes more independent. He will experiment to find out what he can and can't do in his social group – the family. Bad habits, such as play biting, which may have been seen as endearing a few weeks earlier, should be firmly discouraged. Remember to use positive, reward-based training, but make sure your puppy knows that you are the leader and must be respected.

SECOND FEAR-IMPRINT PERIOD (6 to 14 months)

This period is not as critical as the first fear-imprint period, but it should still be handled carefully. During this time your Rottweiler may appear apprehensive, or he may show fear of something familiar. You may feel as if you have taken a backwards step, but if you adopt a calm, positive manner, your Rottweiler will see that there is nothing to be frightened of. Do not make your dog confront the thing that frightens him. Simply distract his attention, and give him something else to think about, such as obeying a simple command, such as "Sit" or "Down". This will give you the opportunity to praise and reward your dog, and will help to boost his confidence.

YOUNG ADULTHOOD AND MATURITY (1 to 4 years)

The timing of this phase depends on the size of the dog: the bigger the dog, the later it is. This period coincides with a dog's increased size and strength, mental as well as physical. Some dogs, particularly those with a pushy attitude will test your leadership again and may become aggressive towards other dogs. Firmness and continued training are essential at this time so that your Rottweiler accepts his position in the family pack.

IDEAS FOR SOCIALISATION

When you are socialising your Rottweiler, you want him to experience as many different situations as possible. Try out some of the following ideas, which will ensure your Rottweiler has an all-round education.

If you are taking on a rescued dog and have little knowledge of his background, it is important to work through a programme of socialisation. A young puppy soaks up new experiences like a sponge, but an older dog can still learn. If a rescued dog shows fear or apprehension, treat him in exactly the same way as you would treat a youngster who is going through the second fear-imprint period (see above).

- Accustom your puppy to household noises, such as the vacuum cleaner, the television and the washing machine.
- Ask visitors to come to the door, wearing different types of clothing – for example, wearing

A young Rottweiler soaks up new experiences like a sponge so every new situation is an opportunity to learn about the world he lives in.

A HELPING HAND

There may well be a situation when your Rottweiler comes across something that makes him nervous or fearful. This may occur when he is a young puppy, or sometimes a youngster will become worried about something – such as a man holding an umbrella – when it hasn't bothered him before. In this situation, a Rottweiler will become tense, his body will be rigid and he will stare at whatever is causing him concern.

Regardless of the age of the dog, or the particular situation, your strategy must be to change your Rottweiler's behaviour so that he becomes relaxed and receptive.

For example, if your Rottweiler has suddenly taken exception to a dustbin, go up and touch the bin, showing him there is nothing to fear. Allow your Rottweiler to approach the bin on a loose lead and let him sniff it. Do not make a big fuss, or drag your Rottweiler towards it, otherwise he will think there is something to fear – simply let him investigate so that he makes his own decision and becomes calm and relaxed.

a hat, a long raincoat, or carrying a stick or an umbrella.

- If you do not have children at home, make sure your Rottweiler has a chance to meet and play with them. Go to a local park and watch children in the play area. You will not be able to take your Rottweiler inside the play area, but he will see children playing and will get used to their shouts of excitement.
- Attend puppy classes. These are designed for puppies between the ages of 12 to 20 weeks, and give the pups a chance to play and interact together in a controlled, supervised environment. Your vet will have details of a local class.
- Take a walk around some quiet streets, such as a residential area, so your Rottweiler can get used to the sound of traffic. As he becomes more confident, progress to busier areas.
- Go to a railway station. You don't have to get on a train if you don't need to, but your Rottweiler will have the chance to experience trains, people wheeling luggage, loudspeaker announcements, and going up and down stairs and over railway bridges.
- If you live in the town, plan a trip to the country. You can enjoy a day out and provide an opportunity for your Rottweiler to see livestock, such as sheep, cattle and horses.
- One of the best places for socialising a dog is at a country fair. There will be crowds of people, livestock in pens, tractors, bouncy castles, fairground rides and food stalls.
- When your dog is over 20 weeks of age, find a training class for adult dogs. You may find that your local training class has both puppy and adult classes.

TRAINING CLUBS

There are lots of training clubs to choose from. Your vet will probably have details of clubs in your area, or you can ask friends who have dogs if they attend a club. Alternatively, use the internet or contact the Kennel Club to find out more information. But how do you

A training class will teach your Rottweiler to work with you despite the distraction of other dogs.

know if the club is any good?

Before you take your dog, ask if you can go to a class as an observer and find out the following:

• What experience does the instructor(s) have?
• Do they have experience with Rottweilers?
• Is the class well organised, and are the dogs reasonably quiet? (A noisy class indicates an unruly atmosphere, which will not be conducive to learning.)
• Are there are a number of classes to suit dogs of different ages and abilities?
• Are positive, reward-based training methods used?
• Does the club train for the Good Citizen Scheme (see page 111)?

If you are not happy with the training club, find another one. An inexperienced instructor who cannot handle a number of dogs in a confined environment can do more harm than good.

THE ADOLESCENT ROTTWEILER

It happens to every dog – and every owner. One minute you have an obedient well-behaved youngster, and the next you have a boisterous adolescent who appears to have forgotten everything he learnt. This applies equally to males and females, although the type of adolescent behaviour, and its onset, varies between individuals.

In most cases a Rottweiler male will hit adolescence at around 11 months, although it may be a couple of months earlier. The male is very slow to mature, and behaviour may remain challenging and unsettled until he is around two years old. Female Rottweilers show adolescent behaviour as they approach their first season. Behaviour may be increasingly influenced by hormonal changes from five months onwards. The timing varies between individuals and between different breeding lines.

In reality, adolescence is not the nightmare period you may imagine, if you see it from your Rottweiler's perspective. Just like a teenager, an adolescent Rottweiler feels the need to flex his muscles and challenge the status quo. He may become disobedient and break house rules as he tests your authority and your role as leader. Your response must be firm, fair and consistent. If you show that you are a strong leader (see page 88) and are quick to reward good behaviour, your Rottweiler will accept you as his protector and provider.

An adolescent Rottweiler may attempt to challenge your authority, but this is easily counteracted with positive, reward-based training.

WHEN THINGS GO WRONG

Positive, reward-based training has proved to be the most effective method of teaching dogs, but what happens when your Rottweiler does something wrong and you need to show him that his behaviour is unacceptable? The old-fashioned school of dog training used to rely on the powers of punishment and negative reinforcement. A dog who raided the bin, for example, was smacked. Now we have learnt that it is not only unpleasant and cruel to hit a dog, it is also ineffective. If you hit a dog for stealing, he is more than likely to see you as the bad consequence of stealing, so he may raid the bin again, but probably not when you are around. If he raided the bin some time before you discovered it, he will be even more confused by your punishment, as he will not relate your response to his 'crime'.

A more commonplace example is when a dog fails to respond to a recall in the park. When the dog eventually comes back, the owner puts the dog on the lead and goes straight home to punish the dog for his poor response. Unfortunately, the dog will have a different interpretation. He does not think: "I won't ignore a recall command because the bad consequence is the end of my play in the park." He thinks: "Coming to my owner resulted in the end of playtime – therefore coming to my owner has a bad consequence, so I won't do that again."

There are a number of strategies to tackle undesirable behaviour – and they have nothing to do with harsh handling.

Ignoring bad behaviour: A lot of undesirable behaviour in young Rottweilers is related to their sheer physical size. Behaviour that was considered cute in a puppy suddenly gets out of hand when the dog becomes full size.

For example, a young Rottweiler that repeatedly jumps up at visitors will eventually knock someone over unless he is stopped. In this case, the Rottweiler is seeking attention, and so the best plan is to ignore him. Do not look at him, do not speak to him, and do not push him down – all these actions are rewarding for your Rottweiler. However, when he has all four feet on the ground, he gets loads of attention. He links the action with the consequence, and chooses the action that is most rewarding.

You will find that this strategy works well with all attention-seeking behaviour, such as barking, whining or scrabbling at doors. Being ignored is a worst-case scenario for a Rottweiler, so remember to use it as an effective training tool.

Stopping bad behaviour: There are occasions when you want to call an instant halt to whatever it is your Rottweiler is doing. He may have just jumped on the sofa, or you may have caught him red-handed in the rubbish bin. He has already committed

Behaviour that may have been acceptable in a puppy can be positively dangerous when a Rottweiler is fully grown.

the 'crime', so your aim is to interrupt his behaviour and to redirect his attention.

The most effective method is to attach a houseline to your Rottweiler's collar. This is a 3-4 ft (0.91-1.21 m) line, which is like a lead without the loop on the end. This means that it can be safely attached to the dog's collar while he is in the house, and he will not get tangled up. The big advantage is that you can correct your Rottweiler without becoming confrontational.

If, for example, you discover your Rottweiler lying on the sofa, you can simply pick up the houseline and lead him away.

You do not have to shout at him or grab his collar. Remain calm and neutral so that the Rottweiler does not feel he has to defend himself. Say "No" in a quiet voice so he understands that he is not allowed on the sofa, and then ask him to do a simple exercise, such as a Sit or a Down, so you can reward desirable behaviour.

PROBLEM BEHAVIOUR

If you have trained your Rottweiler from puppyhood, survived his adolescence and established yourself as a fair and consistent leader, you will end up with a brilliant companion dog. The Rottweiler is a challenging dog to own, but if you gain his respect, he will not seek to thwart your authority.

However, problems may arise unexpectedly, or you may have taken on a rescued Rottweiler that has established behavioural problems. If you are worried about your Rottweiler and feel out of your depth, do not delay in seeking professional help. This is readily available, usually through a referral from your vet, or you can find out additional information on the internet (see Appendices for web addresses).

An animal behaviourist will have experience in tackling problem behaviour and will be able to help both you and your dog.

ROUGH PLAY

It is heartbreaking when the dog you have brought into your family becomes a problem. But in most cases, it is the owner who has got things wrong. A Rottweiler puppy is like a sweet teddy bear, but he is not a cuddly toy and should not be treated as one. He needs appropriate training and guidance so that he understands the world he lives in.

One of the most common mistakes, which can have terrible consequences, is the way you play with your Rottweiler. The Rottweiler is a very physical dog; he was bred to drive cattle and, when needed, he had the power and strength to pin a bullock to the ground. He also has strong guarding instincts and will become defensive if he feels threatened.

It is vital to understand a Rottweiler's temperament from the moment a new puppy arrives in your house. It is all too easy to

Play must be carefully controlled so that the Rottweiler understands the 'rules'.

enjoy a rough and tumble game with a puppy, but before you know it, you could have a very large dog towering over you, fully convinced that he has the upper hand. This is not a breed to play macho games with – you will end up the loser in a situation that could become highly dangerous. The golden rule is: never wrestle or play rough house with a Rottweiler.

When your puppy is small, take the following steps to teach him safe play:

• Put your puppy on a lead and introduce him to a tug toy.

• Give him a game of tug to the count of 10 and then put your foot on his lead, go limp, but do not let go of the toy.
• Ask the puppy to give up the toy, using a command such as "Thank you". This is better than using a command such as "Leave", which is more likely to be spoken in a harsh tone of voice.
• As you have your foot on his lead, the puppy cannot run off with the toy, and as you have stopped playing with him, the fun is over. In a moment or two, he will drop the toy out of frustration and this gives you the opportunity to pick it up and praise him. You can also reward him with a food treat, making sure you throw it on the floor.

This scenario will have to be repeated regularly before your puppy is willing to give up his toy. It is important that once you have stopped the game, you remain as neutral as possible. The game should come to a complete halt, and he will get no further attention until he has dropped the toy.

A well-socialised Rottweiler will be calm and relaxed in the company of other dogs.

PLAYING WITH OTHER DOGS

As we have seen, a Rottweiler's intentions can be misunderstood by other dogs, as his body language can be intimidating. Problems can also arise because a Rottweiler will naturally play rough. Again, this is a result of his physique coupled with the inherited behaviour resulting from pushing and driving cattle. A large dog, such as a Mastiff or a Boxer, may be happy to play rough, but this behaviour must be inhibited if your Rottweiler is going to socialise with other breeds.

The best plan is to take your Rottweiler to puppy socialisation classes and to supervise play sessions in the following way:

- Allow your Rottweiler puppy to play with another pup for a count of 10.
- Call your puppy to you and ask

him to "Sit" for a treat.
- Praise him, let him calm down, and then let him play again for a count of 10.
- Repeat this three or four times, ensuring that your puppy does not get too aroused or over-excited.

If you keep working on this, your Rottweiler will learn that you control play sessions, and you can call a verbal halt to them at any time you wish.

LEADERSHIP CHALLENGE

If you have trained and socialised your Rottweiler correctly, he will know his place in the family pack and will have no desire to challenge your authority. As we have seen, adolescent dogs test the boundaries, and this is the time to enforce all your earlier training so your Rottweiler accepts that he is not top dog.

The Rottweiler is often referred to as a dominant breed, but in reality his behaviour is pragmatic. He asks the question: are you weak or are you strong? He will look at a situation and if he sees he has the advantage – he will take it. Challenging behaviour can be nipped in the bud in puppyhood, but if you have taken on a rescued dog who has not been trained and socialised, or if you have let your adolescent Rottweiler rule the roost, you may find you have problems with a dog who thinks he has the upper hand. This type of behaviour is expressed in many different ways, which may include the following:

- Showing lack of respect for your personal space. For example, your dog will barge through doors ahead of you or jump up at you.
- Getting up on to the sofa or

your favourite armchair, and growling when you tell him to get back on the floor.
- Becoming possessive over a toy, or guarding his food bowl by growling when you get too close.
- Growling when anyone approaches his bed or when anyone gets too close to where he is lying.
- Ignoring basic obedience commands.
- Showing no respect to younger members of the family, pushing amongst them and completely ignoring them.
- Male dogs may start marking (cocking their leg) in the house.
- Aggression towards people (see page 110).

If you see any of these signs, you need to adopt a clear and positive approach. Although you need to be firm, you also need to use positive training methods so that your Rottweiler is rewarded for the behaviour you want. In this way, his 'correct' behaviour will be strengthened and repeated.

There are a number of steps you can take to lower your Rottweiler's status. They include:
- Go back to basics and hold daily training sessions. Make sure you have some really tasty treats, or find a toy your Rottweiler really values and

This Rottweiler has full respect for his owner, and is not seeking to barge ahead.

only bring it out at training sessions. Run through all the training exercises you have taught your Rottweiler. Make a big fuss of him and reward him when he does well. This will reinforce the message that you are the leader and that it is rewarding to do as you ask.
- Teach your Rottweiler something new. This can be as simple as learning a trick, such as shaking paws or a 'high five'. Having something new to think about will mentally stimulate your Rottweiler, and he will benefit from interacting with you.
- Be 100 per cent consistent with all house rules – your Rottweiler must never sit on the sofa and you must never allow him to jump up at you.
- If your Rottweiler is guarding his food bowl, you need to

adopt a training protocol over a number of weeks so that you change his attitude with regard to people approaching his bowl. Take an empty bowl and drop one piece of food into it at a time. In this way you become a predictor for receiving food rather than a potential threat. However, if you have taken on a rescued dog who has serious food guarding problem, enlist the help of an experienced professional trainer, as there is a serious risk of getting bitten in this difficult situation.
- Do not let your Rottweiler barge through doors ahead of you or leap from the back of the car before you release him. You may need to put your dog on the lead and teach him to "Wait" at doorways, and then reward him for letting you go through first.

If your Rottweiler is progressing well with his retraining programme, think about getting involved with a dog sport, such as agility or competitive obedience. This will give your Rottweiler a positive outlet for his energies. However, if your Rottweiler is still seeking to be dominant, or you have any other concerns, do not delay in seeking the help of an animal behaviourist.

LEARNING SOMETHING NEW

Channel your Rottweiler's energies into a positive training exercise so you can reward him for desirable behaviour. This Rottweiler is being taught the Sendaway. This exercise is used in competitive obedience, but you can adapt it to home use by 'sending' your Rottweiler to his bed.

The Rottweiler is directed to a chosen target – in this case it is a pole with a toy attached.

The Rottweiler gets to the target.

He is trained to go into the Down position as soon as he reaches the target.

SEPARATION ANXIETY

The Rottweiler is not a particularly needy dog and if he is brought up to accept short periods of separation from his owner, there is no reason why he should become anxious. A new puppy should be left for short periods on his own, ideally in a crate where he cannot get up to any mischief. It is a good idea to leave him with a boredom-busting toy (see page 58) so he will be happily occupied in your absence. When you return, do not rush to the crate and make a huge fuss. Wait a few minutes, and then calmly go to the crate and release your dog, telling him how good he has been. If this scenario is repeated a number of times, your Rottweiler will soon learn that being left on his own is no big deal.

AGGRESSION

Aggression is a complex issue, as there are different causes and the behaviour may be triggered by numerous factors. It may be directed towards people, but far more commonly it is directed towards other dogs. Aggression in dogs may be the result of:

- **Defensive behaviour:** This may be induced by fear, pain or punishment.
- **Territory:** A dog may become aggressive if strange dogs or people enter his territory (which is generally seen as the house and garden).
- **Intra-sexual issues:** This is aggression between sexes – male-to-male or female-to-female.
- **Parental instinct:** A mother dog may become aggressive if she is protecting her puppies.

Contrary to common belief,

aggression is very rarely the result of dominance; anxiety is a far more likely cause. A dog who has been well socialised (see page 100) and has been given sufficient exposure to other dogs at significant stages of his development will rarely be aggressive. A well-bred Rottweiler that has been reared correctly should not have a hint of aggression in his temperament. Obviously, if you have taken on an older, rescued dog, you will have little or no knowledge of his background, and if he shows signs of aggression, the cause will need to be determined. In most cases, you would be well advised to call in professional help if you see aggressive behaviour in your dog; if the aggression is directed towards people, you should seek immediate advice. This behaviour can escalate very quickly and could lead to disastrous consequences.

NEW CHALLENGES

If you enjoy training your Rottweiler, you may want to try one of the many dog sports that are now on offer. The Rottweiler thrives on mental stimulation, and specialist training is an excellent way to channel his energies.

GOOD CITIZEN SCHEME

This is a scheme run by the Kennel Club in the UK and the American Kennel Club in the USA. The schemes promote responsible ownership and help you to train a well-behaved dog

The versatile Rottweiler will excel in many of the specialist canine sports.

who will fit in with the community. The schemes are excellent for all pet owners, and they are also a good starting point if you plan to compete with your Rottweiler when he is older. The KC and the AKC schemes vary in format. In the UK there are three levels – bronze, silver and gold – with each test becoming progressively more demanding. In the AKC scheme there is a single test.

Some of the exercises include:
• Walking on a loose lead among people and other dogs.
• Recall amid distractions.
• A controlled greeting where dogs stay under control while owners meet.
• The dog allows all-over

grooming and handling by its owner, and also accepts being handled by the examiner.
• Stays, with the owner in sight, and then out of sight.
• Food manners, allowing the owner to eat without begging, and taking a treat on command.
• Sendaway – sending the dog to his bed.

The tests are designed to show the control you have over your dog, and his ability to respond correctly and remain calm in all situations. The Good Citizen Scheme is taught at most training clubs. For more information, log on to the Kennel Club or AKC website (see Appendices).

SHOWING

In your eyes, your Rottweiler is the most beautiful dog in the world – but would a judge agree? Showing is a highly competitive sport and the expense of travelling to shows and entries has to be taken into consideration. However, many owners get bitten by the showing bug, and their calendar is governed by the dates of the top showing fixtures.

To be successful in the show ring, a Rottweiler must conform as closely as possible to the Breed Standard, which is a written blueprint describing the 'perfect' Rottweiler (see Chapter Seven). To get started you need to buy a puppy that has show potential and then train him to perform in the ring. A Rottweiler will be expected to stand in show pose, gait for the judge in order to show off his natural movement, and to be examined by the judge. This involves a detailed hands-on examination, so your Rottweiler must be bombproof when handled by strangers.

Many training clubs hold ringcraft classes, which are run by experienced showgoers. At these classes, you will learn how to handle your Rottweiler in the ring, and you will also find out about rules,

procedures and show ring etiquette.

The best plan is to start off at some small, informal shows where you can practise and learn the tricks of the trade before graduating to bigger shows. It's a long haul starting in the very first puppy class, but the dream is to make your Rottweiler up into a Show Champion.

COMPETITIVE OBEDIENCE

Border Collies and German Shepherds dominate this sport, but there is no doubt that the Rottweiler has the intelligence to do well in competitive obedience; the challenge is producing the accuracy that is demanded. The classes start off being relatively easy and become progressively more challenging with additional exercises and the handler giving minimal instructions to the dog.
Exercises include:

- **Heelwork:** Dog and handler must complete a set pattern on and off the lead, which includes left turns, right turns, about turns, and changes of pace.
- **Recall:** This may be when the handler is stationary or on the move.
- **Retrieve:** This may be a dumbbell or any article chosen by the judge.
- **Sendaway:** The dog is sent to a designated spot and must go into an instant Down until he is recalled by the handler.
- **Stays:** The dog must stay in the Sit and in the Down for a set amount of time. In advanced classes, the handler is out of sight.

Scent: The dog must retrieve a single cloth from a pre-arranged pattern of cloths that has his owner's scent, or, in advanced classes, the judge's scent. There may also be decoy cloths.

- **Distance control.** The dog must execute a series of moves (Sit, Stand, Down) without moving from his position and with the handler at a distance.

Does your Rottweiler have what it takes to make his mark in the show ring?

THE RETRIEVE

This is one of the exercises required in competitive obedience.

The handler throws the dumbbell. The dog must wait until he is told to go and "Fetch".

The dog must pick up the dumbbell cleanly.

The dog returns to the handler.

The dumbell is presented to the handler. The exercise is finished when the dog returns to the Heel position.

The Rottweiler was bred to be an active working dog, and he is more than capable of taking on the challenge of agility.

Even though competitive obedience requires accuracy and precision, make it fun for your Rottweiler, with lots of praise and rewards so that you motivate him to do his best. Many training clubs run advanced classes for those who want to compete in obedience, or you can hire the services of a professional trainer for one-on-one sessions.

AGILITY

This fun sport has grown enormously in popularity over the past few years. If you fancy having a go, make sure you have good control over your Rottweiler and keep him slim. Agility is a very physical sport, which demands fitness from both dog and handler. If you want your Rottweiler to compete in agility, do not put him at risk by allowing him to carry excess weight.

In agility competitions, each dog must complete a set course over a series of obstacles, which include:
• Jumps (upright hurdles and long jump)
• Weaves
• A-frame
• Dog walk
• Seesaw
• Tunnels (collapsible and rigid)
• Tyre

Dogs may compete in Jumping classes, with jumps, tunnels and weaves, or in Agility classes, which have the full set of equipment. Faults are awarded for poles down on the jumps, missed contact points on the A-frame, dog walk and seesaw, and refusals. If a dog takes the wrong course, he is eliminated. The winner is the dog that completes the course in the fastest time

with no faults. As you progress up the levels, courses become progressively harder with more twists, turns and changes of direction.

If you want to get involved in agility, you will need to find a club that specialises in the sport (see Appendices). You will not be allowed to start training until your Rottweiler is 12 months old, and you cannot compete until he is 18 months old. This rule is for the protection of the dog, who may suffer injury if he puts strain on bones and joints while he is still growing.

WORKING TRIALS

This is a very challenging sport, but it is ideally suited to the multi-talented Rottweiler. The sport consists of three basic components:
• **Control:** Dog and handler must

complete obedience exercises, but the work does not have to be as precise as it is in competitive obedience. In the advanced classes, manwork (where the dog works as a guard/ protection dog) is a major feature.

- **Agility:** The dog must negotiate a 3 ft (0.91 m) hurdle, a 9 ft (2.75 m) long jump, and a 6 ft (1.82 m) upright scale, which is the most taxing piece of dog equipment.
- **Nosework:** The dog must follow a track that has been laid over a set course. The surface may vary, and the length of time between the track being laid and the dog starting work is increased in the advanced classes.

Tracking is one of the three elements involved in working trials.

The ladder of stakes are: Companion Dog, Utility Dog, Working Dog, Tracking Dog and Patrol Dog. In the US, tracking is a sport in its own right, and is very popular among Rottweiler owners.

If you want to get involved in working trials, you will need to find a specialist club or a trainer that specialises in training for working trials. For more information, see Appendices.

SCHUTZHUND

Schutzhund is another popular sport in which many Rottweilers participate, particularly in the breed's native Germany. The name comes from the German word meaning 'protection dog'. Schutzhund originated in Germany to test the temperament and ability of the German Shepherd Dog, ensuring only quality dogs were bred from. Today it is practised worldwide. There are three disciplines involved in Schutzhund – tracking, obedience and protection. In effect, Schutzhund is a 'triathlon' for working dogs, and, as a result of his working heritage, the Rottweiler acquits himself very well in this sport.

FLYBALL

Flyball is a team sport; the dogs love it, and it is undoubtedly the nosiest of all the canine sports! Four dogs are selected to run in a relay race against an opposing team. The dogs are sent out by their handlers to jump four hurdles, catch the ball from the flyball box, and then return over the hurdles. At the top level, this sport is fast and furious, and although it is dominated by Border Collies, reliable Rottweilers can make a big contribution. This is particularly true in multibreed competitions where the team is made up of four dogs of different breeds, and only one can be a Border Collie or a Working Sheepdog. Points are awarded to dogs and teams. Annual awards are given to top dogs and top teams, and milestone awards are given out to dogs as they attain points throughout their flyballing careers.

SUMMING UP

The Rottweiler is a breed to be reckoned with. He is loving, affectionate, and highly intelligent. In the right hands, he is an outstanding companion dog, but it is vital that you keep your half of the bargain. Spend time socialising and training your Rottweiler so that he respects your authority and understands his place in the family. If you put in the time and effort, you will be rewarded with a magnificent companion who will always be a credit to you and an ambassador for the breed.

THE PERFECT ROTTWEILER

The first Rottweiler Breed Standard was published in 1901 by the International Club for Leonbergers and Rottweiler Dogs. This Standard allowed for the base colour of the Rottweiler to be other than black and also permitted white markings on the chest and legs. The German Rottweiler Club was formed in 1907, and other Rottweiler breed clubs were formed in Germany soon afterwards. It was soon realised that the Rottweiler needed one strong club to take the breed forward, and it was in 1921 that the clubs combined and formed the Allgemeiner Deutscher Rottweiler Klub (ADRK). In 1924, in its desire for consistency in breed type, the ADRK published a Breed Standard in which only black was recognised as the base colour with red and yellow markings.

CURRENT BREED STANDARDS

Today, we have Rottweiler Breed Standards published by the Federation Cynologique Internationale (FCI), which has 80 member countries, the American Kennel Club (AKC), the Canadian Kennel Club (CKC), and the Kennel Club in Britain (KC). In general terms, these Standards do not vary too much from each other, but a key difference is that the KC Standard is the only one that does not have disqualifying faults. The FCI has the most comprehensive Standard. This is not surprising, as it is the breed's country of origin that establishes the FCI Standard so, in effect, the FCI Breed Standard for the Rottweiler is the ADRK Breed Standard.

What becomes apparent in the Breed Standards is that the Rottweiler is a breed without exaggerations, and it is important that we keep this in mind. Too often, we see fashions creeping in, such as over-angulation on hindquarters and excessively long necks, and these are often viewed as virtues. The Breed Standard describes the essential characteristics of a breed and we should strive to adhere to the Standard whether as a breeder or a judge.

INTERPRETATION AND ANALYSIS

GENERAL APPEARANCE

KC
Above average size, stalwart dog. Correctly proportioned, compact and powerful form, permitting great strength, manoeuvrability and endurance.

AKC
The ideal Rottweiler is a medium large, robust and

Ch. Chesara Dark Charles: An outstanding Rottweiler, typifying the size, strength and power of the breed.

powerful dog, black with clearly defined rust markings. His compact and substantial build denotes great strength, agility and endurance. Dogs are characteristically more massive throughout with larger frame and heavier bone than bitches. Bitches are distinctly feminine, but without weakness of substance or structure.

FCI
The Rottweiler is a medium to large size, stalwart dog, neither heavy nor light and neither leggy nor weedy. His correctly

proportioned, compact and powerful build leads to the conclusion of great strength, agility and endurance.

This part of the Breed Standard is often overlooked, but it is very important, as this is the first key test for breed type. We are looking for an above average size, stalwart dog with a compact and powerful form. The Rottweiler is not a giant breed, as some believe, but he should be robust and strong. The FCI Standard clearly states that he should not be heavy, light, leggy or weedy. We are also reminded

that he should be capable of manoeuvrability and endurance, which is essential for his role as a working dog.

CHARACTERISTICS AND TEMPERAMENT

KC
Appearance displays boldness and courage. Self-assured and fearless. Calm gaze should indicate good humour. Good natured, not nervous, aggressive or vicious; courageous, biddable, with natural guarding instincts.

AKC

The Rottweiler is basically a calm, confident and courageous dog with a self-assured aloofness that does not lend itself to immediate and indiscriminate friendships. A Rottweiler is self-confident and responds quietly and with a wait-and-see attitude to influences in his environment. He has an inherent desire to protect home and family, and is an intelligent dog of extreme hardness and adaptability with a strong willingness to work, making him especially suited as a companion, guardian and general all-purpose dog.

The behavior of the Rottweiler in the show ring should be controlled, willing and adaptable, trained to submit to examination of mouth, testicles, etc. An aloof or reserved dog should not be penalized, as this reflects the accepted character of the breed. An aggressive or belligerent attitude towards other dogs should not be faulted.

A judge shall excuse from the ring any shy Rottweiler. A dog shall be judged fundamentally shy if, refusing to stand for examination, it shrinks away from the judge. A dog that in the opinion of the judge menaces or threatens him/her, or exhibits any sign that it may not be safely approached or examined by the judge in the normal manner, shall be excused from the ring. A dog that in the opinion of the judge

The calm gaze indicates good humour.

attacks any person in the ring shall be disqualified.

FCI

Good natured, placid in basic disposition and fond of children, very devoted, obedient, biddable and eager to work. His appearance is natural and rustic, his behaviour self assured, steady and fearless. He reacts to his surroundings with great alertness.

The Rottweiler should be good natured and willing to follow instructions, but he should still be capable of performing his role as the guardian of his family and property. He should display confidence and alertness, almost aloofness. Contrary to the picture painted of the Rottweiler in certain sections of the media, he

should not be vicious and, equally as undesirable, he should not be nervous.

HEAD AND SKULL

KC

Head medium length, skull broad between ears. Forehead moderately arched as seen from side. Occipital bone well developed but not conspicuous. Cheeks well boned and muscled but not prominent. Skin on head not loose, although it may form a moderate wrinkle when attentive. Muzzle fairly deep with topline level, and length of muzzle in relation to distance from well defined stop to occiput to be as 2 to 3. Nose well developed with proportionately large nostrils, always black.

EYES
Medium size, almond-shaped, dark brown in colour, light eye undesirable, eyelids close fitting.

EARS
Pendant, small in proportion rather than large, set high and wide apart, lying flat and close to cheek.

MOUTH
Teeth strong, complete dentition with scissor bite, i.e. upper teeth closely overlapping lower teeth and set square to the jaws. Flews black and firm, falling gradually away towards corners of mouth, which do not protrude excessively.

AKC
Of medium length, broad between the ears; forehead line seen in profile is moderately arched; zygomatic arch and stop well developed with strong broad upper and lower jaws. The desired ratio of backskull to muzzle is 3 to 2. Forehead is preferred dry, however some wrinkling may occur when dog is alert. *Expression* is noble, alert, and self-assured. *Muzzle:* Bridge is straight, broad at base with slight tapering towards tip. The end of the muzzle is broad with well developed chin. Nose is broad rather than round and always black.

EYES
Of medium size, almond shaped with well fitting lids, moderately deep-set, neither protruding nor receding. The desired color is a uniform dark brown. Serious Faults: Yellow (bird of prey) eyes, eyes of different color or size, hairless eye rim. Disqualification: Entropion. Ectropion.

EARS
Of medium size, pendant, triangular in shape; when carried alertly the ears are level with the top of the skull and appear to broaden it. Ears are to be set well apart, hanging forward with the inner edge lying tightly against the head and terminating at approximately mid-cheek. Serious Faults: Improper carriage (creased, folded or held away from cheek/head).

MOUTH
Lips - Always black; corners closed; inner mouth pigment is preferred dark. Serious Faults - Total lack of mouth pigment (pink mouth). Bite and Dentition: Teeth 42 in number (20 upper, 22 lower), strong, correctly placed, meeting in a scissors bite – lower incisors touching inside of upper incisors. Serious Faults: Level bite; any missing tooth. Disqualifications: Overshot,

The head is broad between the ears; the forehead is moderately arched when seen in profile.

undershot (when incisors do not touch or mesh); wry mouth; two or more missing teeth.

FCI

Skull: Of medium length, broad between the ears. Forehead line moderately arched as seen from the side. Occipital bone well developed without being conspicuous.
Stop: Well defined.
Nose: Nose well developed, more broad than round with relatively large nostrils, always black.
Muzzle: The foreface should appear neither elongated nor shortened in relation to the cranial region. Straight nasal bridge, broad at base, moderately tapered.
Cheeks: Zygomatic arches pronounced.
Skin on the head: Overall tight fitting. When the dog is alert, the forehead may be slightly wrinkled.

EYES

Of medium size, almond shaped, dark brown in colour. Eyelids close fitting.

EARS

Medium-sized, pendant, triangular, wide apart, set on high. With the ears laid forward close to the head the skull appears to be broadened.

MOUTH

Lips: Black, close fitting, corner of the mouth not visible, gum as dark as possible.

Jaws/Teeth: Upper and lower jaw strong and broad. Strong complete dentition (42 teeth) with scissor bite, the upper incisors closely overlapping the lower incisors.

The Rottweiler has often been described as a 'head' breed. While the head is an extremely important characteristic of the breed, there is so much more to him than that. We want a head that is broad and of moderate length. The stop should be well defined but the forehead in profile should not be so steep that it forms a right angle with the muzzle.

The muzzle itself should be deep and should form 40 per cent of the length of the head from the tip of the muzzle to the back of the skull. There has been a trend in Britain over recent years for the muzzle to become shorter and this should cause concern. It would be interesting to apply a skull-measuring device, as used for Breed Suitability Tests on the continent, to determine the correct skull proportions. The cheeks should be well developed. The skin on the head should be tight but may wrinkle slightly when alert.

All the Breed Standards make reference to almond shaped eyes,

The female head has exactly the same proportions as the male head, but on a slightly smaller scale.

dark brown in colour with tight fitting eyelids. Many Rottweiler enthusiasts regard light eyes as a purely cosmetic fault, but the eye colour is an extremely important breed characteristic. You need only refer to the KC Standard which says *'light eye is undesirable'*. The FCI Standard also lists a light eye as a fault and goes further in that a yellow eye is an eliminating fault. Eyes of the correct colour and shape are a key component of the Rottweiler's calm expression.

Ears are important to the head's overall balance and, correctly placed, appear to broaden the width of the skull. The KC Standard makes reference to ears being small in proportion rather than large, but this should not be interpreted as a requirement for ears to be small. There is a clue in that the ears should lie flat and close to the cheek. Ears that are too small will not reach the cheek and rarely lie flat. Both the FCI and AKC Standards ask for ears to be of medium size.

Complete dentition is required – which means 22 lower and 20 upper teeth, with a scissor bite. In order to establish that all 42 teeth are present, a judge has to examine the mouth thoroughly, as some teeth, particularly the third molars on the lower jaw, can only be viewed with the

The teeth meet in a scissor bite with the upper teeth closely overlapping the teeth on the lower jaw.

mouth wide open. The KC Breed Standard does not specifically identify missing teeth as being undesirable and, in the British show ring, dogs have won top honours with this fault. However, the situation is completely different elsewhere, with the FCI and CKC Standards declaring that a missing tooth is an eliminating fault. It is a disqualification in the AKC Standard to have two or more missing teeth.

The KC Standard makes reference to black flews, but does not comment on the pigment inside the mouth. It is not surprising, therefore, that many British judges pay little or no attention to bright mouth pigment. All the other Standards require dark gums or inner mouth pigment, and a bright pink mouth is considered a serious fault.

NECK

KC

Of fair length, strong, round and very muscular. Slightly arched, free from throatiness.

AKC

Powerful, well muscled, moderately long, slightly arched and without loose skin.

FCI

Strong, of fair length, well muscled, slightly arched, free from throatiness, without dewlap.

The neck should be of moderate length, strong, slightly arched without loose skin on the throat. The use of the words 'of fair length' in the KC Breed Standard could be misinterpreted to mean that the neck should be fairly long. Necks that are excessively long or short are not only incorrect but ruin the overall balance of the Rottweiler in profile.

FOREQUARTERS

KC

Shoulders well laid back, long and sloping, elbows well let down, but not loose. Legs straight, muscular, with plenty of bone and substance. Pasterns sloping slightly forward.

AKC

Shoulder blade is long and well laid back. Upper arm equal in length to shoulder blade, set so elbows are well under body. Distance from withers to elbow and elbow to ground is equal. Legs are strongly developed with straight, heavy bone, not set close together. Pasterns are strong, springy and almost perpendicular to the ground. Feet are round, compact with well arched toes, turning neither in nor out. Pads are thick and hard. Nails short, strong and black. Dewclaws may be removed.

FCI

Forequarters: Seen from the front, the front legs are straight and not placed too closely to each other. The forearm, seen from the side, stands straight. The slope of the shoulder blade is about 45 degrees to the horizontal. Shoulders: Well laid back. Upper arm: Close fitting to the body. Forearm: Strongly developed and muscular. Pasterns: Slightly springy, strong, not steep.

A correct forequarters assembly is essential for the Rottweiler to

The front legs are straight and muscular with plenty of substance.

function effectively. The shoulders should be well laid back, and the upper arm should be of equal length to bring the elbows under the body. The bone on the forelegs should be strong. The pasterns should be slightly sloping and these act as effective shock absorbers for the dog in action.

A common fault is for the upper arm to be short and steep, which places the elbow forward; very often this coincides with upright pasterns.

BODY

KC

Chest roomy, broad and deep with well sprung ribs. Depth of brisket will not be more, and not much less, than 50 per cent of shoulder height. Back straight, strong and not too long, ratio of shoulder height to length of body should be as 9 is to 10, loins short, strong and deep, flanks not tucked up. Croup of proportionate length, and broad, very slightly sloping.

AKC

Topline: The back is firm and level, extending in a straight line from behind the withers to the croup. The back remains horizontal to the ground while the dog is moving or standing. *Body:* The chest is roomy, broad and deep, reaching to elbow, with well pronounced forechest and well sprung, oval ribs. Back is straight and strong. Loin is short, deep and well muscled. Croup is broad, of medium length and only slightly sloping. Underline of a mature Rottweiler has a slight tuck-up. Males must have two normal testicles properly descended into the scrotum. *Disqualification:* Unilateral cryptorchid or cryptorchid males.

The height to length proportions of a Rottweiler are 9:10.

FCI

Back: Straight, strong, firm.
Loins: Short, strong and deep.
Croup: Broad, of medium
length, slightly rounded.
Neither flat nor falling away.
Chest: Roomy, broad and deep
(approximately 50 % of the
shoulder height) with well
developed forechest and well
sprung ribs.
Belly: Flanks not tucked up.

The chest should be broad and
deep with well-sprung ribs; the
depth of the chest should be
about 50 per cent of the height at
the shoulder. A dog that is too
deep in chest will look short on
his front legs; conversely, one
that is too shallow will look leggy.
A lack of spring in the ribs will
result in his width of body being
narrow.

The Rottweiler is *not* a square
dog, as his height to length
proportions should be 9:10. His
back should be straight and
strong, the loins should be short
and deep. Long loins can often
result in a tucked-up
undercarriage and affect his
ability to hold a firm backline.
The croup should be broad and
slightly sloping and this is an area
that needs greater attention since
the tail docking legislation. A
short, level croup can produce a
high tail set, something that has
often been forgiven with a
docked tail. This will be
mentioned in 'Tail'.

HINDQUARTERS

KC

Upper thigh not too short,
broad and strongly muscled.

Lower thigh well muscled at
top, strong and sinewy below.
Stifles fairly well bent. Hocks
well angulated without
exaggeration, metatarsals not
completely vertical. Strength
and soundness of hock highly
desirable.

AKC

Angulation of hindquarters
balances that of forequarters.
Upper thigh is fairly long, very
broad and well muscled. Stifle
joint is well turned. Lower
thigh is long, broad and
powerful, with extensive
muscling leading into a strong
hock joint. Rear pasterns are
nearly perpendicular to the
ground. Viewed from the rear,
hind legs are straight, strong
and wide enough apart to fit
with a properly built body.

FCI

Seen from behind, legs straight
and not too close together.
When standing free, obtuse
angles are formed between the
dog's upper thigh and the hip
bone, the upper thigh and the
lower thigh and the metatarsal.
Upper thigh: Moderately long,
broad and strongly muscled.
Lower thigh: Long, strongly and
broadly muscled at top, sinewy.
Hocks: Sturdy well angulated
hocks; not steep.

The angulation on the
hindquarters should balance the
forequarters. Stifles should be
fairly well bent and hocks well
angulated – again, there should
be no exaggeration here. The rear

pasterns, or metatarsals, should not be completely vertical and this reflects the slightly sloping pasterns on the front. Both the upper thighs and lower thighs (the muscled area between the stifle and hock joint) should be strongly muscled.

All the Breed Standards ask for the hocks to be strong and the KC Standard stresses this point by stating *'strength and soundness of hock highly desirable'*.

FEET

KC
Strong, round and compact with toes well arched. Hindfeet somewhat longer than front. Pads very hard, toenails short, dark and strong. Rear dewclaws removed.

AKC
Feet are somewhat longer than the front feet, turning neither in nor out, equally compact with well arched toes. Pads are thick and hard. Nails short, strong, and black. Dewclaws must be removed.

FCI
Front feet: Round, tight and well arched; pads hard; nails short, black and strong.

The angulation of the hindquarters should balance that of the forequarters.

Hindfeet: Slightly longer than the front feet. Toes strong, arched, as tight as front feet.

Correct feet are important to a working breed. The Rottweiler is an endurance trotter and should be capable of working for long periods over a variety of terrains. Compact feet with well-arched toes will assist in keeping the nails short and strong. A flatter foot will result in the toenails growing forward and having minimal contact with the ground and the nails may require regular clipping. All the Standards ask for

pads to be hard, as this provides greater protection for the feet.

It is a requirement of all the Standards that the rear dewclaws should be removed; in fact, many puppies are born without rear dewclaws. It should be noted that the removal of front dewclaws is optional for individual breeders.

TAIL

KC
Previously customarily docked. Docked: Docked at first joint. Strong and not set too low. Normally carried horizontally but slightly above horizontal when dog is alert. Undocked: Strong and not set too low. Normally carried horizontally but slightly above horizontal when dog is alert. May hang when dog is at rest.

FCI
In natural condition, level in extension of the upperline; at ease may be hanging.

AKC
Tail docked short, close to body, leaving one or two tail vertebrae. The set of the tail is more important than length. Properly set, it gives an

UNDERSTANDING TAIL CARRIAGE

1. Normal tail carriage (acceptable in the show ring)
2. Tail carriage when dog's attention has been alerted (acceptable in the show ring)
3. Tail carriage when dog is happy and alert (acceptable in the show ring)
4. Tail curled over the back is a conformation fault and is thus unacceptable.

Illustration courtesy of Allgemeiner Deutscher Rottweiler Klub (ADRK).

impression of elongation of **topline; carried slightly above horizontal when the dog is excited or moving.**

The introduction of Animal Welfare legislation around the world has resulted in tail docking being banned in many countries. The KC, FCI and CKC Breed Standards have all been amended to accommodate the Rottweiler with an undocked tail. At the time of writing the AKC Breed Standard does not contain a description of a full tail.

The KC Breed Standard is quite brief with regard to the Rottweiler tail; the FCI Standard includes eliminating faults, such as *'kink tail, ring tail, with strong lateral deviation'*. (See Faults, page 130.)

The strength of the tail is important; a weak 'whippy' tail looks very unpleasant and affects the overall balance of the Rottweiler. Tail set will be apparent at an early stage, and it is here where greater emphasis

may need to be placed on a correctly sloping croup.

Tail carriage will present the greatest challenge, as this has not been an issue during the years of tail docking. There is little doubt that we will see a large number of dogs with a high tail carriage, and this will result in a variety of tail types from sabre to those more akin to the Spitz breeds. Breeders and judges in many countries have a lot to learn about the Rottweiler tail; it is very mobile and can quickly change from a hanging position on the stand to a high carriage on the move. Consistency in tail type will take many years to improve.

GAIT/MOVEMENT

KC
Conveys an impression of supple strength, endurance and purpose. While back remains firm and stable there is a powerful hindthrust and good stride. First and foremost, movement should be harmonious, positive and unrestricted.

AKC
The Rottweiler is a trotter. His movement should be balanced, harmonious, sure, powerful and unhindered, with strong forereach and a powerful rear drive. The motion is effortless, efficient, and ground-covering. Front and rear legs are thrown neither in nor out, as the imprint of hind feet should touch that of forefeet. In a trot the forequarters and hindquarters are mutually coordinated while the back remains level, firm and relatively motionless. As speed increases the legs will converge under body towards a center line.

FCI
The Rottweiler is a trotting dog. In movement the back remains firm and relatively stable. Movement harmonious, steady, full of energy and unrestricted, with good stride.

The Rottweiler should move with suppleness, strength and purpose.

Two key ingredients of good movement are correct conformation and mental attitude. We have spoken about the desired angulation and musculature on the fore and hindquarters, and a back that is straight and strong but, in order to move with purpose, the dog must have the desire to do so.

We should never lose sight of the original role of the Rottweiler, herding cattle over great distances for long periods, hence the need for strength and endurance. The drive comes from his powerful hindquarters, and this means that good front extension is necessary so that his movement is balanced and harmonious. At the same time the back should remain firm. A Rottweiler moving correctly will cover the ground in an effortless

manner and is a joy to behold.

The KC and FCI Standards make no reference to movement as seen coming and going. The AKC and CKC Standards require front and rear legs not to be thrown in or out and acknowledge that the legs will converge towards a centre line as speed increases.

COAT

KC
Consists of top coat and undercoat. Top coat is of medium length, coarse and flat. Undercoat, essential on the neck and thighs, should not show through top coat. Hair may also be a little longer on the back of the forelegs and breechings. Long or excessively wavy coat highly undesirable.

Bred to drive cattle in all weathers, the Rottweiler needed a coat to keep him warm and dry.

more visible than black undercoat, and it can look untidy, but it is better to have some undercoat present than none at all.

Long and excessively wavy coats are regarded as serious faults. Such coats are eliminating faults in the FCI Standard and considered as highly undesirable in the KC Standard. A long coat is a disqualification in the AKC Standard and open, excessively short or curly coats and total lack of undercoat are classified as serious faults.

COLOUR

KC

Black with clearly defined markings as follows: a spot over each eye, on cheeks, as a strip around each side of muzzle, but not on bridge of nose, on throat, two clear triangles on either side of the breast bone, on forelegs from carpus downward to toes, on inside of rear legs from hock to toes, but not completely eliminating black from back of legs, under tail. Colour of markings from rich tan to mahogany and should not exceed 10 per cent of body colour. White marking is highly undesirable. Black pencil markings on toes are desirable. Undercoat is grey, fawn, or black.

AKC

Always black with rust to mahogany markings. The demarcation between black and rust is to be clearly defined. The

AKC

Outer coat is straight, coarse, dense, of medium length and lying flat. Undercoat should be present on neck and thighs, but the amount is influenced by climatic conditions. Undercoat should not show through outer coat. The coat is shortest on head, ears and legs, longest on breeching. The Rottweiler is to be exhibited in the natural condition with no trimming. Fault: Wavy coat. Serious Faults: Open, excessively short, or curly coat; total lack of undercoat; any trimming that alters the length of the natural coat. Disqualification: Long coat.

FCI

Hair: The coat consists of a top coat and an undercoat. The top coat is of medium length, coarse, dense and flat. The undercoat must not show through the top coat. The hair is a little longer on the hindlegs.

Again we should understand the original function of the Rottweiler to appreciate the importance of a correct coat. In addition to being able to drive cattle, he was exposed to the elements and needed a coat to keep him warm and dry.

All the Standards are consistent and require a coat that consists of a top and undercoat. The top coat should be of medium length, flat and coarse. Unfortunately, too many Rottweilers have short coats that lack undercoat and this is often overlooked in the show ring as some perceive this to be smart looking; this should not be the case.

All Standards also require that the undercoat does not show through the top coat, this is often the case when a dog is moulting. Clearly a fawn or grey will be markings should be located as follows: a spot over each eye; on cheeks; as a strip around each side of muzzle, but not on the bridge of the nose; on throat; triangular mark on both sides of prosternum; on forelegs from carpus downward to the toes; on inside of rear legs showing down the front of the stifle and broadening out to front of rear legs from hock to toes, but not completely eliminating black from rear of pasterns; under tail; black penciling on toes. The undercoat is gray, tan, or black. Quantity and location of rust markings is important and should not exceed ten percent of body color. Serious Faults: Straw-colored, excessive, insufficient or sooty markings; rust marking other than described above; white marking any place on dog (a few rust or white hairs do not constitute a marking). Disqualifications: Any base color other than black; absence of all markings.

FCI
Colour: Black with clearly defined markings of a rich tan on the cheeks, muzzle, throat, chest and legs, as well as over both eyes and under the base of the tail.

The base colour of the Rottweiler should always be black. His markings should be clearly defined and can range from rich tan to mahogany. The KC and AKC Standards state that the markings should not exceed 10

The rich tan-coloured markings should be clearly defined.

per cent of the body colour. It is very difficult to measure what constitutes 10 per cent with the markings being distributed in sections on various parts of the body. As these markings are a key breed characteristic, it is important that there is a clear demarcation between the colours. Sooty markings and excessive markings are considered to be serious faults in the FCI and KC Standards.

It is not unusual for Rottweilers to be born with white markings, usually on the chest, and this is a throwback to the breed's association with Swiss breeds, such as the Bernese Mountain Dog (see Chapter Two: The First Rottweilers). White markings are regarded as highly undesirable in the KC Standard and are a serious

fault in the AKC and CKC Standards. The FCI Standard goes further and lists white markings as an eliminating fault.

SIZE

KC
Dogs height at shoulder: between 63-69 cms (25-27 ins); bitches between 58-64 cms (23-25 ins). Height should always be considered in relation to general appearance.

AKC
Dogs: 24 inches to 27 inches. Bitches: 22 inches to 25 inches, with preferred size being mid-range of each sex. Correct proportion is of primary importance, as long as size is within the standard's range.

FCI

Height at withers: For males is 61-68 cm. 61-62 cm is small; 63-64 cm is medium height; 65-66 cm is large-correct height; 67-68 cm is very large. Weight: approximately 50 kg.

Height at withers: For bitches is 56-63 cm. 56-57 cm is small; 58-59 cm is medium height; 60-61 cm is large-correct height; 62-63 cm is very large. Weight: approximately 42 kg.

The length of the body, measured from the sternum (breast-bone) to the ischiatic tuberosity, should not exceed the height at the withers by, at most, 15 per cent.

There appears to be some inconsistency in height between the Standards, mainly in relation to the bottom end of the scale. However, all the Standards contain further guidance to assist us when considering the height. The FCI Standard breaks down the height range into four categories with dogs 65-66 cms and bitches 60-61 cms being graded as large-correct height. The other Standards add considerations such as proportions or general appearance rather than just height alone.

In the show ring, each dog is given a 'hands on' examination so that the judge can make a thorough assessment.

FAULTS

KC

Any departure from the foregoing points should be considered a fault and the seriousness with which the fault should be regarded should be in exact proportion to its degree and its effect upon the health and welfare of the dog.

Male animals should have two apparently normal testicles fully descended into the scrotum.

AKC

The foregoing is a description

of the ideal Rottweiler. Any structural fault that detracts from the above described working dog must be penalized to the extent of the deviation. Disqualifications: Entropion, ectropion. Overshot, undershot (when incisors do not touch or mesh); wry mouth; two or more missing teeth. Unilateral cryptorchid or cryptorchid males. Long coat. Any base color other than black; absence of all markings. A dog that in the opinion of the judge attacks any person in the ring.

FCI

Any departure from the foregoing points should be considered a fault and the seriousness with which the fault should be regarded should be in exact proportion to its degree.

General appearance: Light, weedy, leggy appearance. Light in bone and muscle.

Head: Hound-type head. Narrow, light, too short, long or coarse head. Flat forehead (lack of stop or too little stop).

Foreface: Long or pointed

muzzle; split nose; Roman nose (convex nasal bridge) or dish-faced (concave nasal bridge); aquiline nose; pale or spotted nose (butterfly nose).

Lips: Pendulous, pink or patchy; corner of lips visible.

Jaws: Narrow lower jaw.

Bite: Pincer bite.

Cheeks: Strongly protruding.

Eyes: Light, deep set. Also too full and round eyes; loose eye-lids.

Ears: Set on too low, heavy, long, slack or turned backwards. Also flying ears or ears not carried symmetrically.

Neck: Too long, thin, lacking muscle. Showing dewlap or throaty.

Body: Too long, too short or too narrow.

Back: Too long, weak; sway-back or roach back.

Croup: Too sloping, too short, too flat or too long.

Chest: Flat ribbed or barrel shaped. Too narrow behind.

Tail: Set on too high or too low.

Forequarters: Narrow or crooked front legs. Steep shoulder placement. Loose or out at elbow. Too long, too short or too straight in upper arm. Weak or steep pastern. Splayed feet. Too flat or too arched toes. Deformed toes. Light coloured nails.

Hindquarters: Flat thighs, hocks too close, cow hocks or barrel hocks. Joints with too little or too much angulation. Dewclaws.

Skin: Wrinkles on head.

It is the dog who comes closest to the 'perfect' Rottweiler, as described in the Breed Standard, that will be placed by the judge.

Coat: Soft, too short or too long. Wavy coat; lack of undercoat.

Colour: Markings of incorrect colour, not clearly defined. Markings which are too spread out.

Eliminating Faults:

General: Distinct reversal of sexual type, i.e. feminine dogs or masculine bitches.

Teeth: Overshot or undershot bite, wry mouth; lack of one incisor tooth, one canine, one premolar and one molar.

Eyes: Entropion, ectropion, yellow eyes, different coloured eyes.

Tail: Kink tail, ring tail, with strong lateral deviation

Hair: Definitely long or wavy coat.

Colour: Dogs which do not show the typical Rottweiler colouring of black with tan markings. White markings.

Behaviour: Anxious, shy, cowardly, gun-shy, vicious, excessively suspicious, nervous animals.

N.B.: Male animals must have two apparently normal testicles fully descended into the scrotum.

SUMMARY

The aim of the Breed Standard is to convey a mental picture of the ideal Rottweiler, in order to maintain consistency of temperament and type.

Without the Standard, breeders and judges would undoubtedly apply their own criteria and there would soon be many variations in the appearance, characteristics and temperament of the dog.

HAPPY AND HEALTHY

Chapter 8

The Rottweiler is a most handsome dog with a life-span often running into double figures, provided his needs are met. The Rottweiler is renowned as a brave companion and a willing friend on a non-conditional basis. He will, however, rely on you for food and shelter, accident prevention and medication in order to remain fully fit and healthy.

There are a few genetic conditions that occur in the Rottweiler. They will be covered in depth later in the chapter.

ROUTINE HEALTH CARE

VACCINATION

There is much debate over the issue of vaccination at the moment. Timing of the final part of the initial vaccination course for a puppy and the frequency of subsequent booster vaccinations

are both under scrutiny. An evaluation of the relative risk for each disease plays a part, depending on the local situation.

Many owners think that the actual vaccination is the protection, so that their puppy can go out for walks as soon as he or she has had the final part of the puppy vaccination course. This is not the case.

The rationale behind vaccination is to stimulate the immune system into producing protective antibodies, which will be triggered if the patient is subsequently exposed to that particular disease. This means that a further one or two weeks will have to pass before an effective level of protection will have developed.

Vaccines against viruses stimulate longer-lasting protection than those against bacteria, whose effect may only persist for a matter of months in

some cases. There is also the possibility of an individual failing to mount a full immune response to a vaccination; although the vaccine schedule may have been followed as recommended, that particular dog remains vulnerable.

An individual's level of protection against rabies, as demonstrated by the antibody titre in a blood sample, is routinely tested in the UK in order to fulfil the requirements of the Pet Travel Scheme (PETS). This is not the case with other individual diseases to gauge the need for booster vaccination or to determine the effect of a course of vaccines; instead, your veterinary surgeon will advise a protocol based upon the vaccines available, local disease prevalence, and the lifestyle of you and your dog.

It is worth remembering that maintaining a fully effective level of immune protection against the

disease appropriate to your locale is vital. These are serious diseases, which may result in the demise of your dog, and some may have the potential to be passed on to his human family (so-called zoonotic potential for transmission). This is where you will be grateful for your vet's own knowledge and advice.

The American Animal Hospital Association laid down guidance at the end of 2006 for the vaccination of dogs in North America. Core diseases were defined as distemper, adenovirus, parvovirus and rabies. So-called non-core diseases are kennel cough, Lyme disease and leptospirosis. A decision to vaccinate against one or more non-core diseases will be based on an individual's level of risk, determined on lifestyle and where you live in the US.

Do remember, however, that the booster visit to the veterinary surgery is not 'just' for a booster.

I am regularly correcting my clients when they announce that they have 'just' brought their pet for a booster. Instead, this appointment is a chance for a full health-check and evaluation of how a particular dog is doing. After all, we are all conversant with the adage that a human year is equivalent to seven canine years.

There have been attempts in recent times to re-set the scale for two reasons: small breeds live longer than giant breeds, and dogs are living longer than previously. I have seen dogs of 17 and 18 years of age, but to say a dog is 119 or 126 years old is plainly meaningless. It does emphasise the fact, though, that a dog's health can change dramatically over the course of a single year because dogs age at a far greater rate than humans.

For me as a veterinary surgeon, the booster vaccination visit is a challenge: how much can I find

of which the owner was unaware, such as rotten teeth or a heart murmur? Even monitoring bodyweight year upon year is of use, because bodyweight can creep up, or down, without an owner realising. Being overweight is unhealthy, but it may take an outsider's remark to make an owner realise that there is a problem. Conversely, a drop in bodyweight may be the only pointer to an underlying problem.

The diseases against which dogs are vaccinated include:

ADENOVIRUS
Canine Adenovirus 1 (CAV-1) affects the liver (hepatitis) and the classic 'blue eye' appearance in some affected dogs, whilst CAV-2 is a cause of kennel cough (see later). Vaccines often include both canine adenoviruses.

DISTEMPER
Also called 'hardpad' from the

Kennel cough is highly infectious and spreads rapidly among dogs that live together.

characteristic changes to the pads of the paws. Distemper has a worldwide distribution, but fortunately vaccination has been very effective at reducing its occurrence. It is caused by a virus and affects the respiratory, gastro-intestinal (gut) and nervous systems, so it causes a wide range of illnesses. Fox and urban stray dog populations are most at risk, and therefore responsible for local outbreaks.

KENNEL COUGH
Also known as infectious tracheobronchitis, Bordetella bronchiseptica is not only a major cause of kennel cough but also a common secondary infection on top of another cause. Being a bacterium, it is susceptible to treatment with

appropriate antibiotics, but the immunity stimulated by the vaccine is therefore short-lived (six to 12 months).

This vaccine is often in a form to be administered down the nostrils in order to stimulate local immunity at the point of entry, so to speak. Do not be alarmed to see your veterinary surgeon using a needle and syringe to draw up the vaccine because the needle will be replaced with a special plastic introducer, allowing the vaccine to be gently instilled into each nostril. Dogs generally resent being held more than the actual intra-nasal vaccine, and I have learnt that covering the patient's eyes helps greatly.

Kennel cough is, however, rather a catch-all term for any

cough spreading within a dog population not just in kennels but also between dogs at a training session or breed show, or even mixing out in the park. Many of these infections may not be B. bronchiseptica but other viruses, for which one can only treat symptomatically. Parainfluenza virus is often included in a vaccine programme because it is a common viral cause of kennel cough.

Kennel cough can seem alarming. There is a persistent cough accompanied by the production of white frothy spittle, which can last for a matter of weeks, during which time the patient is highly infectious to other dogs. I remember when it ran through our five Border Collies – there were white

135

patches of froth on the floor wherever you looked! Other features include sneezing, a runny nose, and eyes sore with conjunctivitis. Fortunately, these infections are generally self-limiting, most dogs recovering without any long-lasting problems, but an elderly dog may be knocked sideways by it, akin to the effects of a common cold on a frail elderly person.

LEPTOSPIROSIS

Contact with rats and their urine is the common way that dogs contract this disease, also known as Weil's disease in humans. This is a zoonotic disease with implications for all those in contact with an affected dog.

The UK National Rodent Survey 2003 found a wild brown rat population of 60 million in the UK, equivalent at the time to one rat per person. I have heard it said that, in the UK, you are never more than a foot (30 cm) from a rat! This means that there is as much a risk for the Rottweiler living with a family on the edge of a town as there is for the Rottweiler living in the countryside.

The situation in the US is less clear-cut. Blanket vaccination

At the present time, Lyme disease is rarely seen in the UK.

against leptospirosis is not considered necessary because it only occurs in certain areas, so you must be guided by your veterinarian.

LYME DISEASE

Lyme disease is a bacterial infection transmitted by hard ticks. It is therefore found in those specific areas of the US where ticks are found, such as north-eastern states, some southern states, California and the upper Mississippi region. It does also occur in the UK but at a low level so vaccination is not

routinely offered.

Clinical disease is manifested primarily as limping due to arthritis, but other organs affected include the heart, kidneys and nervous system. It is readily treatable with appropriate antibiotics, once diagnosed, but the causal bacterium, Borrelia burgdorferi, is not cleared from the body totally and will persist.

Prevention requires both vaccination and tick control, especially as there are other diseases transmitted by ticks. Ticks carrying B. burgdorferi will transmit it to humans as well, but an infected dog cannot pass it to a human.

PARVOVIRUS

Parvovirus appeared in the late 1970s, when it was thought that the UK's dog population would be decimated by it. This was a notion that terrified me at the time but which did not fortunately happen on the scale envisaged. Occurrence is mainly low now, thanks to vaccination. It is also occasionally seen in the elderly unvaccinated dog.

Young Rottweilers seem to have a unique susceptibility to parvovirus infection, sadly often ending fatally. For this reason, an additional later vaccination at around the age of 16 weeks may be recommended by your veterinary surgeon. This is in an attempt to establish better protective immunity than seems to be attained by Rottweilers with a standard two-injection primary vaccination course. Their resistance to other diseases appears to be the same as in other breeds, fortunately.

RABIES

Rabies is another zoonotic disease and there are very strict control measures in place. Vaccines were once only available in the UK on an individual basis for dogs being taken abroad. Pets travelling into the UK had to serve six months' compulsory quarantine so that any pet incubating rabies would be identified before release back into the general population. Under the Pet Travel Scheme, provided certain criteria are met (visit the DEFRA website for up-to-date information – www.defra.gov.uk) then dogs can re-enter the UK without being quarantined.

Dogs to be imported into the US have to show that they were vaccinated against rabies at least 30 days previously; otherwise, they have to serve effective internal quarantine for 30 days

The breeder will have started a worming programme, which you will need to continue with your puppy.

from the date of vaccination against rabies, in order to ensure they are not incubating rabies. The exception is dogs entering from countries recognised as being rabies-free, in which case it has to be proved that they lived in that country for at least six months beforehand.

PARASITES

A parasite is defined as an organism deriving benefit on a one-way basis from another, the host. It goes without saying that it is not to the parasite's advantage to harm the host to

such an extent that the benefit is lost, especially if it results in the death of the host.

This means a dog could harbour parasites, internal and/or external, without there being any signs apparent to the owner. Many canine parasites can, however, transfer to humans with variable consequences, so routine preventative treatment is advised against particular parasites. Just as with vaccination, risk assessment plays a part – for example, there is no need for routine heartworm treatment in the UK (at present), but it is vital in the US and in Mediterranean countries.

INTERNAL PARASITES

Roundworms (nematodes)
These are the spaghetti-like worms, which you may have been unfortunate enough to have seen passed in faeces or brought up in vomit. Most of the deworming treatments in use today cause the adult roundworms to disintegrate, thankfully, so that treating puppies in particular is not as unpleasant as it used to be!

Most puppies will have a worm burden, mainly of a particular roundworm species (Toxocara canis), which reactivates within the dam's tissues during

HEARTWORM (Dirofilaria immitis)

Heartworm infection has been diagnosed in dogs all over the world. There are two prerequisites: presence of mosquitoes and a warm, humid climate.

When a female mosquito bites an infected animal, it acquires D. immitis in its circulating form, as microfilariae. A warm temperature is needed for these microfilariae to develop into the infective third-stage – larvae (L3) – within the mosquitoes, the so-called intermediate host. L3 larvae are then transmitted by the mosquito when it next bites a dog. Therefore, while heartworm infection is found in all the states of the US, it is at differing levels. For example, an occurrence in Alaska is probably a reflection of a visiting dog, having picked up the infection elsewhere.

Heartworm infection is not currently a problem in the UK except for those dogs contracting it while abroad, without suitable preventative treatment. However, global warming, and its effect on the UK's climate, could change that.

It is a potentially life-threatening condition, which, without preventative treatment, can make dogs of all breeds and ages susceptible. The larvae can grow to 14 inches (35.5 cm) within the right side of the heart, causing primarily signs of heart failure and ultimately liver and kidney damage. It can be treated, but prevention is a better plan. In the US, regular blood tests for the presence of infection are advised, coupled with appropriate preventative measures. It is advisable to liaise with your veterinary surgeon.

For dogs travelling to heartworm-endemic areas of the EU, such as the Mediterranean coast, preventative treatment should be started before leaving the UK and maintained during the visit. Again, this is best arranged with your vet.

pregnancy and passes to the foetuses developing in the womb. It is therefore important to treat the dam both during and after pregnancy, as well as the puppies.

Professional advice is to continue worming every month. There are roundworm eggs in the environment and, unless you examine your dog's faeces under a microscope on a very regular basis for the presence of roundworm eggs, you will be unaware of your dog having picked up roundworms, unless he should have such a heavy burden that he passes the adults.

It takes a few weeks from the time that a dog swallows a Toxocara canis roundworm egg to himself passing viable eggs (the pre-patent period). There are deworming products that are active all the time, which will provide continuous protection when administered as often as directed. Otherwise, treating every month will, in effect, cut in before a dog could theoretically become a source of roundworm eggs to the general population. It is the risk to human health that is so important: T. canis roundworms will migrate within our tissues and cause all manner of problems, not least of which is blindness. If a dog has roundworms, the eggs also find their way on to his coat where they can be picked up during stroking and cuddling.

You should always carefully pick up your dog's faeces and dispose of them appropriately, which will not only reduce the chance for environmental contamination with all manner of infections but also make walking more pleasant underfoot.

Tapeworms (cestodes)
When considering the general dog population, the primary source of the commonest tapeworm species will be fleas, which can carry the eggs. Most multi-wormers will be active against these tapeworms, not because they are a hazard to human health but because it is

unpleasant to see the wriggly rice grain tapeworm segments emerging from your dog's back passage while he is lying in front of the fire, and usually when you have guests round for dinner!

There are specific requirements for treatment with praziquantel within 24 to 48 hours of return into the UK under the PETS. This is to prevent the inadvertent introduction of Echinococcus multilocularis, a tapeworm carried by foxes on mainland Europe, which is transmissible to humans, causing serious or even fatal liver disease.

Regular preventative treatment will eliminate the problem of external parasites.

EXTERNAL PARASITES
Fleas

There are several species of flea, which are not host-specific: not only can a dog be carrying cat and human fleas as well as dog fleas, but also the same flea treatment will kill and/or control them all. It is also accepted that environmental control is a vital part of a flea control programme. This is because the adult flea is only on the animal for as long as it takes to have a blood meal and to breed; the remainder of the life cycle occurs in the house, car, caravan, shed...

There is a vast array of flea control products available, with various routes of administration: collar, powder, spray, 'spot-on', oral. Since flea control needs to be applied to all pets in the house (and that is independent of whether they leave the house since fleas can be introduced into the house by other pets and their human owners), it is best to discuss your specific flea control needs with your vet.

Ticks

There were said to be classic pockets of ticks in the UK, such as the New Forest and Thetford Forest, but they are actually found nationwide. The life cycle is curious: each life stage takes a year to develop and move on to the next. Long grass is a major habitat. The vibration of animals moving through the grass will stimulate the larva, nymph or adult to climb up a blade of grass and wave its legs in the air as it 'quests' for a host on to which to latch for its next blood meal. Humans are as likely to be hosts, so ramblers and orienteers are advised to cover their legs when going through rough long grass, tucking the ends of their trousers into their socks.

As well as their physical presence causing irritation, it is the potential for disease transmission that is of concern. A tick will transmit any infection previously contracted while feeding on an animal: for example Borrelia burgdorferi, the causal agent of Lyme disease (see above).

A-Z OF COMMON AILMENTS

ACUTE MOIST DERMATITIS (AMD) OR HOT SPOT

I have seen many Rottweilers with a patch of AMD just below the ear. The skin and overlying fur appear wet, which is due to a sticky discharge caused by the

Keep a close check on your Rottweiler's general condition and then you will spot any problems at an early stage.

infection in the skin. The area is very painful to the touch, so that it is often necessary to sedate the patient before clipping away the fur. A large area of infected skin may be revealed, but removing the fur back to visually healthy skin enables a thorough cleansing of all the affected area. A course of appropriate antibiotic by mouth is often prescribed, together with topical treatment. The response is generally rapid, the infection resolving within 10 to 14 days.

The initial cause may have been an insect sting or an ear infection (see below) stimulating the patient to scratch at his ear and thereby irritating the skin below it. Patient interference does play a role in the development of AMD, a vicious cycle becoming established because the infected area is itchy for the patient. Preventing further scratching and rubbing of the area is paramount for the infection to clear up.

ANAL SACS, IMPACTED

The anal sacs lie on either side of the back passage or anus at approximately four- and eight-o'-clock, if compared with the face of a clock. They fill with a particularly pungent fluid, which is emptied on to the faeces

as they move past the sacs to exit from the anus. Theories abound as to why these sacs should become impacted periodically and seemingly more so in some dogs than others. The irritation of impacted anal sacs is often seen as 'scooting', when the backside is dragged along the ground. Some dogs will gnaw at their back feet or over the rump.

Increasing the fibre content of the diet helps some dogs; in others, there is underlying skin disease. It may be a one-off occurrence for no apparent reason. Sometimes, an infection can become established, requiring antibiotic therapy, which may need to be coupled with flushing out the infected sac under sedation or general anaesthesia. More rarely, a dog will present with an apparently acute-onset anal sac abscess, which is incredibly painful.

BONE TUMOUR

The Rottweiler seems to be afflicted with a higher than expected incidence of osteosarcoma at the end of the long bones of the limbs, and at a relatively young age, often manifesting as a lameness failing to respond to standard treatment of analgesia (pain relief) and rest. I particularly remember one September when, as a practice, we diagnosed four Rottweilers with primary bone tumours.

CANINE ACNE

With an appearance very similar to acne in humans, and found on the muzzle, the Rottweiler is one of the breeds commonly seen with canine acne. Various treatments are used with varying success, often depending on the individual, such as local washing and attention to hygiene.

CRANIAL CRUCIATE LIGAMENT RUPTURE

This is one of a pair of ligaments that cross the stifle or knee joint. Rupture of the cranial cruciate ligament is a common cause of hindlimb lameness in the breed, especially in the young Rottweiler. Neutering seems to increase the susceptibility, although this may reflect weight gain. The Rottweiler is a heavily-built breed which can be very active, exerting extreme forces on their joints.

This is not the place for an in-depth consideration of the biomechanics underlying the rationale for the various surgical procedures performed in an attempt to re-stabilise the stifle, but the after-care by the owner is crucial to the outcome. Strict confinement necessary in conjunction with a controlled, slowly rising plane of lead exercise. During the recovery phase of three to six months, care must be taken to avoid weight

Many Rottweilers enjoy swimming, but beware of ear infection if water gets trapped in the external ear canal.

gain whilst on a reduced regime of exercise. It is not unusual for a Rottweiler to go lame on the other hindlimb a little while later with a cranial cruciate ligament rupture in that stifle, having been bearing a greater proportion of the bodyweight whilst the first stifle was healing.

EAR INFECTIONS

The dog has a long external ear canal, initially vertical then horizontal, leading to the eardrum, which protects the middle ear. If your Rottweiler is shaking his head, then his ears will need to be inspected with an auroscope by a veterinary surgeon in order to identify any cause, and to ensure the eardrum is intact. A sample may be taken

from the canal to be examined under the microscope and cultured to identify causal agents before prescribing appropriate ear drops containing antibiotic, anti-fungal agent and/or steroid. Predisposing causes of otitis externa or infection in the external ear canal include:

- Presence of a foreign body, such as a grass awn
- Ear mites, which are intensely irritating to the dog and stimulate the production of brown wax, predisposing to infection
- Previous infections causing the canal's lining to thicken, narrowing the canal and reducing ventilation
- Swimming – some Rottweilers love swimming, but water trapped in the external ear canal can lead to infection, especially if the water is not clean!

FOREIGN BODIES

Internal: Items swallowed in haste without checking whether they will be digested can cause problems if they lodge in the stomach or obstruct the intestines, necessitating surgical removal. Acute vomiting is the main indication. Common objects I have seen removed include stones from the garden, peach stones, babies' dummies, golf balls, and once a lady's bra...

It is possible to diagnose a dog with an intestinal obstruction across a waiting room from a particularly 'tucked-up' stance and pained facial expression. These patients bounce back from surgery dramatically. A previously docile and compliant obstructed patient will return for a post-operative check-up and literally bounce into the consulting room.

External: Grass seeds are adept at finding their way into orifices such as a nostril, down an ear, and into the soft skin between two digits (toes), whence they start a one-way journey due to the direction of their whiskers. In particular, I remember a grass awn that migrated from a hindpaw, causing abscesses along the way but not yielding itself up until it erupted through the skin in the groin!

GASTRITIS
This is usually a simple stomach upset, most commonly in response to dietary indiscretion. Scavenging constitutes a change in the diet as much as an abrupt switch in the food being fed by the owner. Generally, a day without food, followed by a few days of small, frequent meals of a bland diet (such as cooked chicken or fish or an appropriate prescription diet) should allow the stomach to settle. It is vital to wean the patient back on to routine food or else another bout of gastritis may occur.

JOINT PROBLEMS
It is not unusual for older Rottweilers to be stiff after exercise, particularly in cold weather. This is not really surprising, given that they are a breed with a big frame. Your veterinary surgeon will be able to advise you on ways to help your dog cope with stiffness, not least of which will be to ensure that he is not overweight. Arthritic joints do not need to be burdened with extra bodyweight!

LUMPS
Regularly handling and stroking your dog will enable the early detection of lumps and bumps. These may be due to infection (abscess), bruising, multiplication of particular cells from within the body, or even an external parasite (tick). If you are worried about any lump you find, have it checked by a vet.

OVERWEIGHT
Being overweight does predispose to many other problems, such as diabetes mellitus, heart disease and joint problems. It is so easily prevented by simply acting as your Rottweiler's conscience. Ignore pleading eyes and feed according to your dog's waistline.

Make sure you guard against the dangers of obesity.

The body condition is what matters qualitatively, alongside monitoring that individual's bodyweight as a quantitative measure. The Rottweiler should, in my opinion as a health professional, have at least a suggestion of a waist and it should be possible to feel the ribs beneath only a slight layer of fat.

Neutering does not automatically mean that your Rottweiler will be overweight. Having an ovario-hysterectomy does slow down the body's rate of working, castration to a lesser extent, but it therefore means that your dog needs less food, a lower energy intake. I recommend cutting back a little on the amount of food fed a few weeks before neutering to accustom your Rottweiler to less food. If she looks very slightly underweight on the morning of the operation, it will help the veterinary surgeon as well as giving her a little leeway weight-wise afterwards.

It is always harder to lose weight after neutering than before, because of this slowing in the body's inherent metabolic rate.

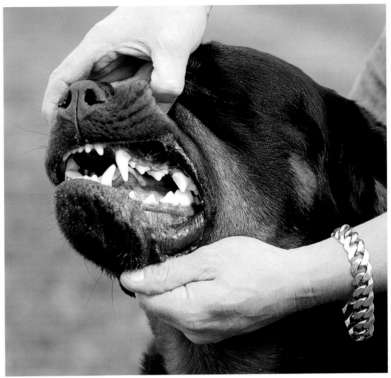

A regime of regular cleaning will ensure healthy teeth and gums.

TEETH

Eating food starts with the canine teeth gripping and killing prey in the wild, incisor teeth biting off pieces of food and the molar teeth chewing it. To be able to eat is vital for life, yet the actual health of the teeth is often overlooked; unhealthy teeth can predispose to disease, and not just by reducing the ability to eat. The presence of infection within the mouth can lead to bacteria entering the bloodstream and then filtering out at major organs, with the potential for serious consequences. That is not to forget that simply having dental pain can affect a dog's well-being, as anyone who has had toothache will confirm.

Veterinary dentistry has made huge leaps in recent years, so that it no longer consists of extraction as the treatment of necessity.

Good dental health lies in the hands of the owner, starting from the moment the dog comes into your care. Just as we have taken on responsibility for feeding, so we have acquired the task of maintaining good dental and oral hygiene. In an ideal world, we should brush our dogs' teeth as regularly as our own. The Rottweiler puppy who finds having his teeth brushed is a huge game and excuse to roll over and over on the ground requires loads of patience, twice a day.

There are alternative strategies, ranging from dental chew-sticks to specially formulated foods, but the main thing is to be aware of your dog's mouth. At least train your puppy to permit full examination of his teeth, which will not only ensure you are checking in his mouth regularly but will also make your vet's job easier when there is a real need for your dog to "Open wide!"

INHERITED DISORDERS

Any individual, dog or human, may have an inherited disorder by virtue of genes acquired from the parents. This is significant not only for the health of that individual but also because of the potential for transmitting the disorder on to that individual's offspring and to subsequent generations, depending on the mode of inheritance.

There are control schemes in place for some inherited disorders. In the US, for example, the Canine Eye Registration Foundation (CERF) was set up by dog breeders concerned about heritable eye disease, and provides a database of dogs who have been examined by diplomates of the American College of Veterinary Ophthalmologists.

There are several major disorders that are thought to be inherited in the Rottweiler. They include, in alphabetical order:

AORTIC STENOSIS

Aortic stenosis is a congenital malformation of the major outflow vessel from the heart, i.e. present at birth.

ECTROPION

Ectropion is a rolling outwards of the eyelids (usually mild), which usually resolves as the dog grows and matures. It may predispose to conjunctivitis but is usually cosmetic and rarely requires corrective surgery (CERF).

ENTROPION

This is an inrolling of the eyelids. There are degrees of entropion, ranging from a slight inrolling to the more serious case requiring surgical correction because of the pain and damage to the surface of the eyeball (CERF).

ELBOW DYSPLASIA

It is commonly the medial coronoid process that is affected in the Rottweiler. Although occurrence within the breed seems to be rising, this could be a reflection of increased use by breeders of screening under the BVA/KC Scheme*. Standard radiographs of both elbows are taken once an individual has passed his first birthday, and each elbow is scored from zero (unaffected) through to 3 (worst). The highest score of the two elbows is given as that dog's score, with breeders being advised to breed only from those with scores of zero or one. An individual can only have his elbows scored once.

HIP DYSPLASIA

This is a malformation of the hip joints, causing pain, lameness and reduced exercise tolerance in the young Rottweiler, and resulting in degenerative joint disease (arthritis) in the older dog. Each hip joint is scored on several features to give a total of zero to 53 from a radiograph taken with the hips and pelvis in a specified position, usually requiring the dog to be sedated, after the age of one year under the BVA/KC Scheme*, from two years of age in the US (OFA**).

*British Veterinary Association/Kennel Club Scheme
**Orthopedic Foundation for Animals, US

Health checks on breeding stock is essential in preventing inherited diseases.

COMPLEMENTARY THERAPIES

Only a few years ago the use of complementary therapies on animals was virtually unknown, but they are now becoming more widespread and more readily available. Just as for human health, I do believe there is a place for alternative therapies, but alongside and complementing orthodox treatment under the supervision of a veterinary surgeon. That is why 'complementary therapies' is a better name.

Because animals do not have a choice, there are measures in place to safeguard their wellbeing and welfare. All manipulative treatment must be under the direction of a veterinary surgeon who has examined the patient and diagnosed the condition that she or he feels needs that form of treatment. This covers physiotherapy, chiropractic, osteopathy and swimming therapy. For example, dogs with arthritis who cannot exercise as freely as they were accustomed will enjoy the sensation of controlled non-weight-bearing exercise in water, and benefit with improved muscling and overall fitness.

All other complementary therapies, such as acupuncture, homoeopathy and aromatherapy, can only be carried out by vets who have been trained in that particular field. Acupuncture is mainly used in dog for pain relief, often to good effect. The needles look more alarming to the owner, but they are very fine

More Rottweiler owners are becoming aware of the benefits of using complementary therapies.

With good care and management your Rottweiler should live a long, happy and healthy life.

and are well tolerated by most canine patients. Speaking personally, superficial needling is not unpleasant and does help with pain relief. Homoeopathy has had a mixed press in recent years. It is based on the concept of treating like with like. Additionally, a homoeopathic remedy is said to become more powerful the more it is diluted.

CONCLUSION
As the owner of a Rottweiler, you are responsible for his care and health. Not only must you make decisions on his behalf, you are also responsible for establishing a lifestyle for him that will ensure he leads a long and happy life.

Diet plays as important a part in this as exercise, for example. Nutritional manipulation has a long history. Formulation of animal feedstuffs is aimed at optimising production from, for example, dairy cattle. For the domestic dog, it is only in recent years that the need has been recognised for changing the diet to suit the dog as he grows, matures and then enters his twilight years. So-called life-stage diets try to match the nutritional needs of the dog as he progresses through life.

An adult dog food will suit the Rottweiler living a standard family life. There are also foods for those Rottweilers tactfully termed as obese-prone, such as those who have been neutered or are less active than others, or simply like their food. Do remember, though, that ultimately you are in control of your Rottweiler's diet, unless he is able to profit from scavenging!

On the other hand, prescription diets are, of necessity, fed under the supervision of a veterinary surgeon because each is formulated to meet the very specific needs of particular health conditions. Should a prescription diet be fed to a healthy dog, or to a dog with a different illness, there could be adverse effects.

It is important to remember that your Rottweiler has no choice. As his owner, you are responsible for any decision made, so it must be as informed a decision as possible. Always speak to your veterinary surgeon if you have any worries about your Rottweiler. He is not just a dog, because he will have become a definite member of the family from the moment you brought him home.

THE CONTRIBUTORS

THE EDITOR
DI McCANN (PARVENU)
Although now retired, Di has competed in several canine disciplines: working trials (qualifying CDex with a Labrador in 1974); gundog working tests; obedience; the show ring. She owned Labradors for 18 years and Rottweilers for 21 years; she has bred several litters using European bloodlines.

Di was Secretary and Founder Member of the Kent, Surrey and Sussex Labrador Retriever Club in the early 1970s; Committee Member of The Rottweiler Club for three years; Secretary of the London and South East Rottweiler Club (LASER) for three years; and Secretary to the national Rottweiler Breed Council for four years. Di is now a Member of the Kennel Club. She awards Challenge Certificates to Rottweilers in the UK and has judged the Championship Show of the Norwegian Rottweiler Klubb.

Di campaigned extensively in Europe and the UK with her male Schipperke – UK Champion/Dutch Champion/Luxembourg Champion/Belgian Champion/International Champion/Junior World Winner ARADET INDIANA JONES. He won a total of 12 CACIBs, 13 CACs, 6 CCs; was Best of Breed at Crufts 2005 and remains the UK's first and only multi-Champion.
See Chapter One: Getting to Know Rottweilers, Chapter Two: The First Rottweilers, Chapter Three: A Rottweiler for your Lifestyle, and Chapter Four: The New Arrival.

JOYCE SUMMERS (NYGRA)
Joyce Summers has had a love of dogs since childhood. Her interest in Rottweilers began in 1969 after she purchased a bitch who finished her show career as CDex and 2 Res.CCs. Joyce bred her first litter in 1972, one dog siring the third ever Working Trial Champion Rottweiler and two breed Champions. Many show winners and obedience and working trials qualifiers have been bred since. The latest litter was born in 2007; this time, of course, the tails were left undocked. In her breeding programme, Joyce's aim is always to produce dual purpose dogs with correct temperament. Joyce is greatly interested in health issues affecting the Rottweiler and would like more breeders to undertake more of the health tests available. She also gives advice on behaviour and training.

Joyce became Treasurer and a Committee member of The Rottweiler Club, the UK's oldest Rottweiler Club, in 1971 and has held that office to the present time.

Joyce has been actively involved in judging the breed. She started judging at Open Shows in 1973, and gave Challenge Certificates for the first time in 1980. This culminated in the honour of judging male Rottweilers at Crufts in 2005. Furthermore, Joyce has passed the Rottweiler Club's Temperament Assessors Course, leaving her qualified to assess all breeds.
See Chapter Five: The Best of Care.

JULIA BARNES
Julia has owned and trained dogs for many years, and is a puppy socialiser for Dogs for the Disabled. A former journalist, she has written many books, including several on dog training and behaviour.

Julia would like to acknowledge the specialist advice given by Nina Bondarenko in writing this chapter. Australian-born Nina Bondarenko BA, SAC has been training animals for more than 30 years, and now resides in the UK. As founding trainer and former Programme Director for the assistance dog charity Canine Partners UK, Nina developed the unique training approach, methodology, techniques and theory of assistance dog training and development of her Puppy Education System of component behaviours and errorless learning principles.

Nina bred, judged, trained and trialled working Rottweilers in Australia, and assesses puppies and dogs for temperament and working aptitude throughout Europe. Author and illustrator of the book on working dogs, *Hearts, Minds and Paws*, she featured in the BBC documentary series *Doghouse* in 2007, and has presented a range of TV series on dog behaviour and training in Australia and the UK.

Dogs trained by Nina have been awarded "Dog of the Millennium", "Pro Dog of the Year Gold Medal", "Assistance Dog of the Year", "Golden Bone" and "Golden Bonio" of the Year, and two dogs have been awarded the "Dicken Medal for Devotion to Duty".

Nina Bondarenko is the Coordinator for Behaviour and Training for the International Detector Dog Congress, and is a consultant for the International Association for Animal Behaviour Consultants.
See Chapter Six: Training and Socialisation.

CHRIS WINDOW (HANBAR)
Chris has been involved with Rottweilers for 30 years and, with his wife Norma, owns the Hanbar kennel. They have owned and bred numerous Rottweiler champions in the UK and abroad. They have also owned and exhibited champions in Finnish Spitz and bred Challenge Certificate-winning Norwegian Buhund. Chris has judged Rottweilers at Championship Show level since 1993 and is scheduled to judge the breed at Crufts in 2012. He also judges Finnish Spitz at the same level.

In recent years, Chris and Norma have taken advantage of the Pet Passport Scheme to introduce new bloodlines to the UK by using overseas stud dogs with considerable success. They have also enjoyed success exhibiting Rottweilers in mainland Europe.
See Chapter Seven: The Perfect Rottweiler

ALISON LOGAN MA VetMB MRCVS
Alison qualified as a veterinary surgeon from Cambridge University in 1989, having been brought up surrounded by all manner of animals and birds in the north Essex countryside. She has been in practice in her home town ever since, living with her husband, two children and Labrador Retriever, Pippin. Writing is increasingly taking up her time at home, contributing on a regular basis to *Veterinary Times*, *Veterinary Nurse Times*, *Dogs Today*, *Cat World* and *Pet Patter*, the PetPlan newsletter. In 1995, Alison won the Univet Literary Award with an article on Cushing's disease, and she won it again (as the Vetoquinol Literary Award) in 2002, writing about common conditions in the Shar-pei. In her spare time, she would like to play piano, take Pippin for day-long walks and work on the garden... but there are not enough hours in the day!
See Chapter Eight: Happy and Healthy.

BIBLIOGRAPHY

The Rottweiler in Word and Picture
Published by the Allgemeine Deutsche Rottweiler Klub E.V. – 1926
(Translation by Mrs. Dudley Zopp, 1970)

Der Rottweiler
Hans Korn (Translation by John Macphail, 1959)

Dogs in Britain
Clifford L. B. Hubbard (MacMillan, 1948)

The Complete Rottweiler
Muriel Freeman (Howell Book House, 1984)

All About the Rottweiler
Mary MacPhail (Pelham Books, 1986)

The Rottweiler
Judy and Larry Elsden (Popular Dogs Publishing, 1987)

The Rottweiler
Jim Pettengell (David & Charles, 1988)

The Heritage of The Dog
Colonel David Hancock (Nimrod Press, 1990)

Rottweilers – An Owner`s Companion
Les Price (Crowood Press, 1991)

The Rottweiler Today
Judy and Larry Elsden (Ringpress Books, 1991)

Give Your Dog a Bone
Dr. Ian Billinghurst – BVSc [Hons], BSc.Agr., Dip.Ed. (Billinghurst, Australia, 1993)

USEFUL ADDRESSES

BREED CLUBS

The Rottweiler Club (RC)
Miss Elizabeth Harrap
Pangora, Crays Pond, Goring Heath,
Reading, Berks, RG8 7SH
Telephone: 01491 680515

British Rottweiler Association (BRA)
Mrs Margaret Yates
1 Albansfield, Pople Street,
Wymondham, Norfolk, NR18 0PR
Telephone: 01953 600602

Midland Rottweiler Club (MRC)
Mrs Jannette Blunden
The Bungalow, Red Barns Lane, Newton,
Alfreton, Derbys, DE55 5SD
Telephone: 01773 590126

Scottish Rottweiler Club (SRC)
Mrs Sharon Brown
7 Hallside Village, Cambuslang,
Glasgow, G72 7XD
Telephone: 01416 418690

South Western Rottweiler Association (SWRA)
Miss Michelle Derbyshire
46 Highworth Road, St. Annes,
Bristol, BS4 4AG
Telephone: 01179 716904

Eastern Counties Rottweiler Club (ECRC)
Mr John MacKenzie
21 Hemp Bridge Close, Selby,
North Yorkshire, YO8 4XJ
Telephone: 01757 705355

London and South East Rottweiler Club (LASER)
Miss Kim Dowsett
7 Heather Drive, Hadleigh, Essex, SS7 2EL
Telephone: 01702 556997

Rottweiler Club of Wales (RCW)
Mr. Graham Lewis
10 Gilfach Road, Tonyrefail,
Mid Glamorgan, CF39 8HE
Telephone: 01443 674103

North of England Rottweiler Club (N of ERC)
Mrs. Jean Stevens
Plas Cae Coch, Trefriw, Conwy. LL27 0JS
Telephone: 01492 641660

KENNEL CLUBS

American Kennel Club (AKC)
5580 Centerview Drive
Raleigh, NC 27606
Telephone: 919 233 9767
Fax: 919 233 3627
Email: info@akc.org
Web: www.akc.org

The Kennel Club (UK)
1 Clarges Street
London, W1J 8AB
Telephone: 0870 606 6750
Fax: 0207 518 1058
Web: www.the-kennel-club.org.uk

ROTTWEILER RESCUE

Rottweiler Welfare
Telephone: 01782 395558 or 01732 841082
Email: rottwelfare25@tiscali.co.uk
Web: www.rottweilerwelfare.co.uk
(Please be prepared to listen to the answerphone
message and have pencil and
pen ready to take careful note of other phone
numbers for you to ring.)

Rottweilers In Need
Telephone: Ann Evans-Wallett 01691 610470
or Sue Lunt 0151 523 3880
Email: rottweilersinneed@talktalk.net
Web: www.rottweilersinneed.co.uk

TRAINING AND BEHAVIOUR

Association of Pet Dog Trainers (APDT)
PO Box 17, Kempsford, GL7 4W7
Telephone: 01285 810811
Email: APDToffice@aol.com
Web: http://www.apdt.co.uk

Association of Pet Behaviour Counsellors (APBC)
PO BOX 46, Worcester, WR8 9YS
Telephone: 01386 751151
Fax: 01386 750743
Email: info@apbc.org.uk
Web: http://www.apbc.org.uk/

ACTIVITIES

Agility Club
http://www.agilityclub.co.uk/

British Flyball Association
PO Box 109, Petersfield, GU32 1XZ.
Telephone: 01753 620110
Fax: 01726 861079
Email: bfa@flyball.org.uk
Web: http://www.flyball.org.uk/

World Canine Freestyle Organisation
P.O. Box 350122, Brooklyn,
NY 11235-2525, USA
Telephone: (718) 332-8336
Fax: (718) 646-2686
Email: wcfodogs@aol.com
Web: www.worldcaninefreestyle.org

Working Trials
www.workingtrials.co.uk

HEALTH

Alternative Veterinary Medicine Centre
Chinham House, Stanford in the Vale,
Oxfordshire, SN7 8NQ
Email: enquiries@bahvs.com
Web: www.bahvs.com

British Association of Veterinary Ophthalmologists (BAVO)
Email: hjf@vetspecialists.co.uk or
secretary@bravo.org.uk
Web: http://www.bravo.org.uk/

British Small Animal Veterinary Association (BSAVA)
Woodrow House, 1 Telford Way, Waterwells
Business Park, Quedgeley,
Gloucestershire, GL2 2AB
Telephone: 01452 726700
Fax: 01452 726701
Email: customerservices@bsava.com
Web: http://www.bsava.com/

British Veterinary Hospitals Association (BHVA)
Station Bungalow, Main Rd, Stocksfield,
Northumberland, NE43 7HJ
Telephone: 07966 901619
Fax: 07813 915954
Email: office@bvha.org.uk
Web: http://www.bvha.org.uk/

Royal College of Veterinary Surgeons (RCVS)
Belgravia House, 62-64 Horseferry Road,
London, SW1P 2AF
Telephone: 0207 222 2001
Fax: 0207 222 2004
Email: admin@rcvs.org.uk
Web: www.rcvs.org.uk

ASSISTANCE DOGS

Canine Partners
Mill Lane, Heyshott, Midhurst,
West Sussex, GU29 0ED
Telephone: 08456 580480
www.caninepartners.co.uk

Dogs for the Disabled
The Frances Hay Centre, Blacklocks Hill
Banbury, Oxon, OX17 2BS
Telephone: 01295 252600
Web: www.dogsforthedisabled.org

Guide Dogs for the Blind Association
Burghfield Common, Reading, RG7 3YG
Telephone: 01189 835555
Web: www.guidedogs.org.uk/

Hearing Dogs for Deaf People
The Grange, Wycombe Road, Saunderton, Princes
Risborough, Bucks, HP27 9NS
Telephone: 01844 348100
Web: hearingdogs.org.uk

Pets as Therapy
3 Grange Farm Cottages, Wycombe Road,
Saunderton, Princes Risborough, Bucks, HP27 9NS
Telephone: 0870 977 0003
Web: http://www.petsastherapy.org/

Support Dogs
21 Jessops Riverside, Brightside Lane, Sheffield, S9 2RX.
Tel: 0870 609 3476
Web: www.support-dogs.org.uk